STRAIGHT TALK
FROM WILD THING

Mitch Williams
with Darrell Berger

TRIUMPH
BOOKS

To my wife, Irene, and my five kids—Damon, Mitch Jr., Nikola, Dallas, and Declan—without them I would have no reason to get out of bed in the morning!

—Mitch Williams

To my favorite teammates: Rick Young, Wally Ely, and Doc, the best outfielding English Shepherd I ever saw.

—Darrell Berger

Library of Congress Cataloging-in-Publication Data

Williams, Mitch, 1964–
  Straight talk from wild thing / Mitch Williams with Darrell Berger.
    p. cm.
  ISBN 978-1-60078-306-7
  1. Williams, Mitch, 1964– 2. Baseball players—United States—Biography.
3. Pitchers (Baseball)—United States—Biography. 4. Sportscasters—United
States—Biography. I. Berger, Darrell, 1948– II. Title.
  GV865.W497A3 2009
  796.357092—dc22
  [B]

                                                        2010001233

This book is available in quantity at special discounts for your group or organization. For further information, contact:

Triumph Books
542 South Dearborn Street
Suite 750
Chicago, Illinois 60605
(312) 939–3330
Fax (312) 663–3557
www.triumphbooks.com

Printed in U.S.A.
ISBN: 978-1-60078-306-7
Design by Patricia Frey
Photos courtesy AP Images unless otherwise indicated.

Contents

Foreword

So, the 1993 season ends with Joe Carter's homer off Mitch. I'm playing first. The first thing I thought to myself was, *Okay, it's over. We had a helluva run.* We finished last the year before. Last. We thought we had a chance to be better, but we had not dreamed of getting as far as we got. We played hard through the last pitch. Mitch put everything he had into that pitch, just like he had all season.

Back in the clubhouse, we tried to get him into the trainer's room, the traditional postgame place to hide from reporters. "You don't have to talk to them," we told him.

He said it was his responsibility, part of what you sign on for when you play. "If I'd have saved the game, or saved the seventh game, I'd be out talking to them," he said. "It's part of the job." My respect for him grew a lot from that experience. Everybody's a great guy when you win. How are you when you lose? We found out how a couple of guys are when they lose. Some guys were not great teammates.

I was very disappointed when the Phillies traded Mitch a few weeks later. I think management panicked. They believed the mythology of the Phillies fans, booing Santa Claus and all. A few people maybe felt that way, but I doubt they were really cheering us on in the first place. The Phillies management underestimated their fans, and they underestimated Mitch Williams.

The first time I saw Mitch was back in spring training of 1982, when we were both part of the San Diego organization. The first thing I noticed was his size. Now there are pitching staffs that could be mistaken for NBA teams, but back then, Mitch's 6'4" was considered tall.

Plus he was young, just a few weeks removed from high school. There were already stories about how hard he threw. I've had the great privilege of taking batting practice from him. When I walked into the cage, the first thing he said was, "Oh, God. I can't pitch to lefties."

When I was at bat against him, my plan was to hit the ball before it hit me. Since we were friends, I knew he was not going to hit me. On purpose. I remember poor Larry Walker. Mitch kept throwing balls over his head. He had nothing against Larry. Mitch said, "His head is like a magnet for my fastball. I feel sorry for the guy."

You could see Mitch's confidence, the lack of fear he had, right from the beginning. A lot of people saw it as being cocky or arrogant. I think that's why neither of us lasted with the Padres. They wanted choirboys, and the only thing Mitch sang was country. They couldn't wait to get me out of there, either. We just didn't conform to what they wanted. They wanted guys who kept an even keel, not guys who got angry, got fired up. We belonged on an East Coast team that had passionate fans and appreciated it in their players. Philadelphia fit just fine.

He's mellowed some now, but Mitch Williams used to do *everything* like his hair was on fire. When you played golf with Mitch, he tried to set a record every time, not for the best score, but for the shortest time it took to play a round. He'd cuss and throw clubs, not because he hit a bad shot, but because the foursome in front of us was taking too long.

This urge to keep moving wasn't just during our playing days, either. It was only a few years ago, after we both had retired, that we had to get to Florida for the Phillies' fantasy camp at the end of January. The plan was to drive straight through from Philadelphia to Florida in my brand-new Cadillac. We left about 8:00 PM.

In Richmond, Virginia, a snowstorm broke like they get about every 20 years. For six hours we drove about 15 mph. There were 18-wheelers passing us left and right, throwing all sorts of crap on my new car. When we got to Florida it looked like it had been sandblasted.

Mitch, in all of his intelligence, at about 3:00 AM with me white-knuckling it all the way, decided he needed to go to a Walmart for a CD. I made the turn, and in doing so, did a 360. Luckily, there were no cars in the parking lot. Because it was *closed*! We almost got totaled so we could find out the 24-hour Walmart was closed for cleaning.

Traveling with Mitch has a few simple steps. You stop for gas. One of you pumps and the other gets chips and Cokes or something. You do not stop to eat. Never. Ever. So when I unclenched my hands from the wheel and finally said, "You know what? I'm going to stop and have a meal," it upended Mitch's universe. It was not his style to stop and eat while traveling.

"Get back in," he said. "I'll drive and you can eat."

"Nope," I said. "I want to sit. I want to relax. I want a real meal. We have plenty of time to get there."

Mitch admitted he was hungry, but he was so pissed that he wouldn't get out of the car. He didn't talk to me for two hours because I stopped and ate.

I love him, though. He was one of the very few players to come visit my parents and me down in West Virginia. Behind those fashionable mullets we used to wear, we were both down-home guys.

We still get together every couple of weeks, and just recently I've noticed that Mitch seems more relaxed, more comfortable. He might stop to eat during an overnight drive in a storm now. He might even spend the night somewhere. Perhaps this has been partly due to his success behind the microphone in Philadelphia and for MLB-TV. I'm not surprised. I've been telling people for years that behind that swagger is one of the funniest guys you will ever meet. He will make just as much fun of himself as he will of you. I'm happy for him.

I'm happy for you, too. Because when you read this book, you are going to get to know the real Mitch Williams.

—John Kruk

Introduction

The Setup Pitch

Hitting a home run in the ninth inning to win the World Series might be the most common dream among American kids for the last hundred years or so.

For me that dream came true, sort of...

I threw the pitch.

Even worse, I threw it while playing for Philadelphia, the city known for having the toughest fans in sports. Everybody knows the lines: Phillies fans boo Santa Claus; they'll boo your wife. Less than two months after Joe Carter hit my fastball for a three-run homer to win the 1993 World Series, I was traded to Houston.

At first you heard it was because the front office was afraid I'd never be able to play in Philadelphia again. So next May, the first time I pitched in Philadelphia as a visiting player, what happened? I got a standing ovation. Why?

I never made any excuses.

Philadelphia teams have lost more games than teams in any other city. For decades, the Phillies and A's (before they moved on to Kansas City and Oakland) were undercapitalized doormats. The Eagles haven't won since 1960. The 76ers have often contended but seldom prevailed—a lot of close but few cigars. The one thing that makes a Phillies fan go nuts is to hear some variation on, "We would have won if only..." So when I lost and said simply, "I lost," the fans accepted it.

When I came into the game to start the ninth inning against the Toronto Blue Jays, I felt fine. I didn't have my best fastball. It was the middle of October. No baseball player has his best anything in the middle of October. Rickey Henderson was the first batter. Of course, he wasn't going fishing for anything, and like a few hundred other pitchers, I walked him.

I got Devon White on a fly, and then Paul Molitor bounced a single to center. I wasn't worried, but I guess I was the only one who wasn't. Next up was Joe Carter. We went to 2–2. I knew what I wanted to do. He was a rarity for a right-handed batter. He could drop the bat head and really power the low inside pitch. For some reason, this is common for lefty power hitters but rare for righties. I wanted to throw him fastballs high and outside. Fans who have seen me pitch over the years know that high and outside was my specialty. Sometimes a little too high or a little too outside, but still, I figured I could get him.

With runners on board I used the slide step, a way of pitching from the stretch that is intended to economize a pitcher's motion, get the ball to the plate faster, and keep runners close. Most pitchers, and I'm no exception, don't like a slide step. Nobody uses it enough to get comfortable with it, and because you don't lean as far back in your motion as usual, you don't get a chance to gather then pause for a split second before getting everything moving in the same direction. You can't get as much on the ball. At the time it was kind of a fad, so the slide step it was.

You don't get as much power from your body using the slide step. A pitcher tends to muscle the ball to the plate, using his arm to generate the power he's not getting from the rest of his body. But when you ask too much of your arm, the tendency is to hold on to the ball too long. That's what I did. I threw the pitch down and in, and Carter took it up and out. I knew the pitch was gone from the sound of the ball hitting the bat. A pitcher knows that sound.

I didn't feel good, but I didn't feel terrible, either. I treated every game the same. Otherwise, a professional athlete will go crazy. There are just too many ups and downs. A lot of fans don't realize this. They seek emotional highs and lows from rooting. It's an outlet for them. The player can't afford to get that emotional.

I treated it like any other game, but nobody else did. I stayed in the locker room for more than an hour answering some of the dumbest questions you can imagine. Looking back, I think that hour had a lot to do with why the Phillies fans never held a grudge against me. I didn't hide. I didn't make excuses.

I learned a lot about taking responsibility for my actions early in life when I wrestled for four years in middle school and high school. All professional athletes ought to spend a year wrestling. It teaches you something. You get pinned; you can't blame the coach. You can't blame your teammates. The guy you are looking for is staring back at you in the mirror.

My wife, Irene, was at the game. She was my fiancée then. Irene had broken her foot before the playoffs. She still had a cast on that was scheduled to come off soon. She wanted me to take it off that night. I sawed it off using nothing but a kitchen knife! I guess you could say I had some nervous energy that night.

The questions never ended. The media was everywhere I went. I just kept answering their questions and lived my life. What else was there to do? It was a game. I lost. Move on.

On December 2, I moved on to Houston, traded for Doug Jones, Jeff Juden, a good reliever who had as many miles on him as I did, and a huge young pitcher with potential. The Phillies front office never explained whether they traded me because they thought the fans would kill me, or because they thought my arm was dead and the hitters would kill me. Either way, I was dead as a Phillie.

Turns out I was pretty much dead as a major-league pitcher, too. I never pitched another complete season. It wasn't so much my arm as that I had no right leg. I'd had five or six surgeries on my right knee. Almost as many pitching careers are ended by legs as by arms.

My arm and leg weren't the only things that were gone. My heart just wasn't in it anymore. What had been a joy for me for so many years had become just a job. I retired and spent the next four years just taking it easy on my ranch.

I played too much golf, then got heavily into team roping. I found it a challenge and a great physical and competitive outlet, though I'd never done it before. I was pretty good at it, but eventually I wanted to go back to work.

Former Phillies player and current ESPN baseball commentator John Kruk and I put together a few shows for local Philadelphia television. We did about nine shows, shot in a local bar. They went over pretty well, but the station couldn't pay us anything. I took a job managing in the minors at Atlantic City.

From there I worked in marketing for Trump Marina Casino in Atlantic City, later moving to the MGM Mirage. Then I did some personal appearances in the greater Philadelphia area.

The fans and I got along, then came radio and television. From the very beginning, it felt right. It wasn't a matter of the fans "forgiving me," because I don't think they ever blamed me. Okay, maybe the ones throwing the rocks against my house in 1993 blamed me, but not many did or still do.

I never made any excuses, and I always left everything I had on the field. That's all any fan can ask. Maybe standing in front of my locker that night for an hour answering anything anybody asked was the beginning of the Phillies fans trusting me. They knew, like Howard Cosell years ago, that I would "tell it like it is."

I never thought talking baseball or taking fans inside the game would be my strong suit, but here I am. I do a pregame show for TBS and a postgame show for Comcast. I'm on radio 610-WIP AM every week with Angelo Cataldi, and I host "The Wild Pitch" on the Phillies' radio broadcast station, 1210 WPHT-AM. I got in on the ground floor of the MLB television network. Now my pitches have gone beyond the broadcast booth and studios to come to you from the pages of this book. I am writing about what I've seen in the game of baseball over the past 25 or so years with special emphasis on the Phillies, naturally.

I saw every Philadelphia game in 2008 from spring training through the World Series. I knew this team was going to be a good one, but how good? The hitting would be okay, and I thought the relief core was gong to be fine. Nobody knew for sure what Chad Durbin could do, but Ryan Madson was in a position to be a good setup man, J.C. Romero was solid, and I never questioned that closer Brad Lidge would be anything but excellent, though a lot of people did.

There were questions about the starting pitching beyond Cole Hamels. But they did well, even though Jamie Moyer is 150 years old. Their success was the key to the season. The team started out barely over an underachieving .500. Ryan Howard got off to a terrible start. He became a symbol for what some feared would be yet another Philadelphia team that would leave nothing but excuses.

Early in the season Ryan could not cover the outside corner. It was like the plate was 10 feet wide for him. As the season progressed, he obviously made an adjustment. Watch him closely. If his front foot is hitting the ground as he swings, he's fine. If he swings and the foot is still moving, he won't be able to cover the outside corner. The difference is just the slightest amount of extension with his arms, but for Ryan it is the difference between a home run to left or a swing and a miss. The difference between a Ryan homer and a strikeout is the difference between a disappointing Phillies team and a world championship.

It was a great experience watching every Phillies game in 2008. It's funny, but I might not have shared in it had I struck out Joe Carter with a high outside fastball, as I had intended. The 2009 Phillies found out that the toughest thing in professional sports is to repeat.

Sure, I would have preferred to walk off the field that night in 1993 as a winner, anybody would. But in losing, the fans in Philadelphia got to know me. Maybe they could even relate to my experience. A lot of people have lost things in life worse than a ballgame. Since my days with the Chicago Cubs, I have been known as "Wild Thing." I was one of the few pitchers in major-league history to give up more walks than hits.

I may have thrown a little wild, but I've always talked straight.

Chapter One

The Path to the Show

I am the middle child of three sons. I was born in Santa Ana, California, the biggest city in Orange County, but we moved outside of Portland, Oregon, when I was little. My folks divorced when I was twelve. My older brother and I lived with our father; my younger brother lived with my mother. We still lived fairly close to each other, about a 45-minute drive.

My dad was a machinist in a little shop. In fact, he just retired. He worked with the same guys, more or less, for 31 years. My older brother and I were athletes, but not my younger brother. We never had a lot of money. The only thing we could do that didn't cost money was play catch or pick up a football. That's who we were. We counted on sports.

I wrestled until 10th grade. In ninth grade, I was 5'4" and 105 pounds. In 10th, I shot up to 6'2" and 136 pounds. You might say I was just a little skinny.

I lived for Saturday and Sunday and football. I wanted to play football more than anything. In high school, I was a quarterback and did all the placekicking. I could throw a football 75 yards flat-footed, but I could not run a lick.

What I really wanted to do was play defense. I was undersized, but I'd knock your head off. At one point I became the long snapper on punts, because I was the only one who could do it, and because I loved hitting people. The problem was that I weighed 150 pounds my junior year, and I was 6'2" 160 pounds when I finished high school. I was not going to be a college linebacker.

My older brother was a year ahead of me in high school, and he was getting scouted as a senior. We both threw hard, but the scouts were interested in my brother because he was a senior. Scouts would call the high school and ask who was pitching. They would be told, "Williams," show up, and, naturally, half the time I was the one pitching. So scouts noticed me from the time I was a junior.

My brother signed with the Brewers in 1981. The next year I was drafted. He played six years in the minors, but he never got to the big leagues. He threw harder than I did, but control was his problem. That's right—I wasn't even the hardest thrower or wildest pitcher in my family! He was just never able to get it over consistently enough to get people out.

I was lucky I had Tom House when I got to the Rangers. He was the one who got me throwing enough strikes to have a career. I think Tom could have helped my brother, too. Looking back, he was about the hardest thrower I ever saw. If I saw him today, I could help him. He had pitching coaches who believed if you couldn't get it over, you took a little off. That's not the case. You learn control throwing as hard as you can, or you move on to something else. Once you start taking something off in order to throw strikes, you are throwing away your talent. Learn to control your talent. In the long run, it's actually easier.

Scouts brought their radar guns to my high school games. I had people from everywhere looking at me. I was 17–0 my senior year, but I had no clue who was going to draft me.

When I wasn't pitching, I played first. I led the state in home runs, and I think I still hold the Oregon state record for most home runs in a high school season. I hit about .420, but there was no question I was going to be signed as a pitcher. Another strong arm on the mound is always what every team looks for first.

I turned out to be the 8th-round pick of the San Diego Padres in 1982. I was picked because I was left handed and had good velocity. Three days after I graduated high school, I was in Walla Walla, Washington, a professional baseball player. This was rookie ball, what they call "short A"—because it is for kids like me who just got out of school so we didn't have to wait a whole year to get started or get sent to a team that has been together since April.

Walla Walla is only a couple hundred miles from Portland, but it seemed a world away to me. It only has about 30,000 people now, and in 1982 it was even smaller. Now it has more than a hundred wineries and has become like a Napa Valley of the northwest—but when I played there, the main attractions were onions and the prison. It seemed like most everybody either grew onions or worked at the state prison.

The onions were no joke. The team's biggest promotion of the year was Onion Night, where waitresses walked around the stands with onions cut up on trays. People eat them like apples. In fact, the Walla Walla Sweet Onion is the official vegetable of the state of Washington. Don't let anyone say you don't learn anything in the minors.

The state prison was no joke, either. It contains about 10 percent of the town's population, and every once in a while they hang somebody—Washington is one of two states where that still happens.

I won the "Guess the Crowd" contest 11 times that summer. I wasn't that good a guesser, but I could count faster than anybody else. Each time I won, I got two Ford trucker caps. I won 22 caps that year. Of course, the one thing a baseball player doesn't need is a cap, but in Class A you accept anything anybody gives you. Except for Onion Night, we didn't draw very well.

I was a starter, as I was for almost my entire minor-league career, and was 3–4 that season. I showed enough promise to get promoted to "long A" the next year—which was in Reno, Nevada, for the Padres organization, another not-too-exciting place, but it was Paris compared to Walla Walla.

I didn't do too well there. It was a control thing. I was walking about a batter per inning. It wasn't pretty, so back to low A I went, though by now the team had moved to Spokane, which had been as high as Triple A over the years and is much larger than Walla Walla. They have onions there, too, but they don't stress them as much. I pitched better there and the next year, 1984, I went back to Reno for the entire season.

In the winter of 1984, I was taken in the Rule 5 draft by Texas. That means you go to spring training with the major league club. If they want you, they buy you from your original organization, but they have to keep you on the major league roster. If they don't, they have to give you back. I guess they figured I had a live enough arm, and if by chance I ever learned to throw it over the plate, they might have found a bargain.

The Rangers cut me the final day of spring training. They sent me back to the Padres and traded for me the same night. The Padres got an infielder named Randy Asadoor, who at the time was much more highly touted than I had ever been. He had been a star at Cal State Fresno and had already racked up some decent numbers at Triple A. He only got into 15 games in the big leagues, all with the Padres in 1986. He hit .364 but made five errors, which may account for his short stay in the show.

The Rangers sent me to Salem, Virginia, in the Carolina League, still long A. Some time just past mid-season, I got moved to Tulsa in the Texas League.

Walla Walla, Reno, Salem, and Tulsa are a pretty typical tour of the low minors. The main thing about playing in these places is that you basically have to amuse yourself, because you have no money and the towns are not exactly exciting to young guys. I made $600 a month when I started. That scene in *Bull Durham* where they let the sprinklers run and they slid all over the tarp: that would be the high point of most seasons in Class A.

It is usually not that glamorous. The bus ride from Walla Walla to Bellingham is more than 10 hours, and even though it was pretty far north, it was hot in the summer. Though not nearly as hot as the Carolina League, which was not anywhere near as hot as the Texas League. You don't even want to know how hot the Texas League was. Most leagues have some town that is either in the mountains or on the shore so you can get a little relief. Not in the Texas League. Everywhere was bad.

Nobody spends many seasons in Class A ball. You either get promoted or die career-wise, which is fortunate because nobody wants to spend much time riding those buses to get to those towns. It doesn't take long to begin daydreaming about how wonderful Triple A cities like Toledo and Louisville must be.

There aren't too many guys who, like Rick Porcello, pitch a few months in Florida, then take a regular turn in the big leagues before they can buy a legal beer.

What also doesn't help is that the players' union doesn't include minor leaguers. I can see why they don't. In most unions, you serve as an apprentice and, if you can, work at that job for decades, like my dad in his machine shop. But even the average major-league career is less than four years. The turnover in the minors is way more than that. Most of the players in a minor league union would be gone before their membership cards were ready. So you are really on your own, right at the time when most players are away from home for the first time.

It used to be a source of funny stories, just telling how bad the minor-league playing surfaces were. In the Texas League, the ground was just baked hard as a rock. But when I was a minor league manager in an independent A league a few years back, I was amazed at how good the playing fields had become everywhere.

Those independent leagues are fun for the kids and families, and I'm all for them. They gave me the only chance I ever got to get back in the game. But they are where careers go to die—baseball hospice. The players there want to play one more year before they go back to school or the car wash.

I was with Tulsa long enough to make six starts, then the Rangers sent me to play winter ball in Santurce, Puerto Rico. Santurce always has its own team. It is part of San Juan, almost like Brooklyn is part of New York City. The manager there was Frank Verdi, who seemed like a really old guy to me at the time. In fact, he was about sixty, which seems younger and younger every year.

Frank had a major league career of exactly one Yankees game. He replaced Phil Rizzuto at shortstop for part of a game in 1953. He neither fielded a ball nor came to bat. His minor league managing career lasted decades though, and he helped develop countless players.

His most exciting moment in the field came in 1959 when he was with the Rochester Red Wings, the Cardinals Triple A club down in Havana, against the Sugar Kings, which was a farm team of the Cincinnati Reds. Castro was still in the hills, but revolution was in the air, as was a stray bullet, which glanced off Verdi's helmet liner and caused a shoulder wound—a sore arm that had nothing to do with pitch counts. A year later, the Reds moved their team to Jersey City.

I think Texas told him to just use me and find out what I did best. I started and relieved. One time I pitched two innings late in a game and started the next one! Texas found out I had a good arm. I didn't get sore or stiff, and I could pitch some every day.

So I came to the Rangers' spring training in 1986 looking like I might have the makings of a reliever. I was lucky that there was a youth movement on. Bobby Valentine replaced Doug Rader as manager, and Tom House, who had been a roving instructor with San Diego, replaced Dick Such as pitching coach.

As I will tell everyone who asks, Tom House is responsible for my major league career. He started working with me when I was 17 years old, as soon as I turned pro. He worked with me for years. But it wasn't like he whispered in my ear one day, and suddenly I could throw strikes.

I worked for years, first to just comprehend what House was telling me, and then to do it. It was all mechanical. He changed where I put my hands in the set position. He lowered my hands because of my height, which simplified everything by eliminating some useless motion. I completely stopped throwing out of a windup for the same reason and never went back to one again, ever.

I threw across my body some, and a lot of observers make a big deal out of that, but believe me, every good pitcher that ever lived throws at least a little bit across his body. My motion was a little bit more extreme, but it wasn't so much across my body that I was going to hurt myself. That was Tom's opinion, and it proved correct. Actually, when you throw across your body, you stayed closed longer, which puts less stress on your arm and helps to hide the baseball longer. That's where my deception came in. The hitters knew they were going to get a fastball, but they had a little trouble picking up the ball out of my motion. Needing an extra split second to pick up the ball can mean a ground ball to second instead of a double off the wall.

Once I learned House's lessons, he became like the local mechanic who knows your car and all its funny noises and quirks. He was always there when I needed a tune-up.

Once I got to the Rangers, Charlie Hough helped me a lot. You might wonder what a starting knuckleball pitcher can teach a fast-balling reliever. I learned a lot just talking with him and casually playing catch. It wasn't mechanics or hitters he helped me with. It was more that he had a certain professional way of doing things, just the way he went about his business. He had experience, and seemingly, nothing ever bothered him.

Hough looked like he should be walking behind a plow pulled by a couple of mules, but he was as smart as they come. He was born in Honolulu, so he was one of the few players who traveled *east* to play with the Dodgers. He's now a pitching coach in their minor league system. I wonder if he ever teaches that knuckler to anybody?

How unlikely is it that a guy built like Charlie Hough would be a baseball player? Sometimes guards at the ballpark wouldn't let him in the locker room because they thought he was a writer!

As a veteran on a Rangers team with a lot of young guys, he tried to help everybody. He was around forever, eventually heaving that flutter pitch until he was 46 years old. He started the first game in the history of the Marlins. I loved having him for a team-mate. He kept everybody sharp.

He had a one-liner for every occasion. In Incaviglia's rookie year, Pete was a terrible outfielder. He worked his butt off at it and eventually got pretty good, but because of that first year, a lot of people thought he always stunk in the field, and he didn't.

But in 1986, fly balls were bouncing off his chest. It was rank. On the bus somebody used the phrase "Catch 22." Immediately, Hough stood up and said, "What would Inky catch if you hit him a hundred flies?"

I noticed that during batting practice before every game, he'd do nothing but toss knuckleballs against the outfield fence. One

During the eighth inning of Game 6 of the 1977 World Series, Dodgers pitcher Charlie Hough gave up Reggie Jackson's third homer of the night. His knuckleball allowed him to last more than 20 years in the majors. (AP Images)

day I asked him, "Charlie, why don't you ever shag?" Running down flies and grounders is the time-honored pastime for pitchers during batting practice. He looked at me and just kept lobbing pitches at the fence. He said. "It is always better to look lazy than bad."

He was so lazy he only pitched for 25 years! And after all that work, he was even with the world. He won 216 games, lost 216.

When I wanted to find out about different hitters, I didn't talk to pitchers, I talked to hitters. I found out how they thought. I spent a lot of time with Larry Parrish and Pete O'Brien. I would much rather learn what a hitter is thinking, what his tendencies are, than what a pitcher thinks about that same hitter.

Just because a pitcher can get out a certain hitter with his slider for example, doesn't mean that your slider will get him out. Some hitters just "see" you better than others. Sometimes the angle that your pitches cross the plate just happens to meet the angle where his bat crosses it. That guy will hit you better than another guy, who just happens to swing, most of the time, along a different plane. That's why, if you look at averages of various hitters against me, some very ordinary hitters killed me and some very good hitters were awful. Sometimes it is just a small sample size, not enough at-bats, but just as often it is because of this kind of mechanical coincidence. It is true of every pitcher.

I did pretty well in spring training in 1986. But until you have success at any level of baseball, there is always some doubt, both in your mind and the minds of the coaches, managers, and general managers deciding your fate. And in 1986, I had not had notable success anywhere as a starter, and my career as a reliever was hardly more than an experiment.

Putting extra doubt in my mind was that, in the minors, I saw literally hundreds of talented players who I thought couldn't miss but did. The game from the neck up is the one you have to play, and a lot of players can't. It's not the baseball itself, thinking about the game and learning to compete on the next level, but the discipline and resiliency it takes to survive 10-hour bus trips from Walla Walla to Bellingham on $600 a month.

The talent that finally decides who survives in the major leagues isn't playing talent, it's what a guy does with what he's been given. The mental toughness, the ability to just plain hang in there, is far rarer than the ability to hit or throw a 90-mph fastball.

There is one thing you will hear over and over again when a guy quits pro ball or even gives up a college scholarship: "It wasn't fun anymore." This is the universal copout because they are right; it is not fun. When you begin a professional career, whether you are walking off a high school campus, a college campus, or some dirt field with chicken-wire fences in the Dominican Republic, you are going from being the stuff, the big guy, the hero, to "what have you done today?"

You are going from a team, even a league, where nobody had your ability, to a situation where you might not stack up. The reason it's not fun anymore is that you aren't the best one on the field. This is a sudden, unpleasant reality. I was 42–5 in high school and didn't lose a game as a senior—then I walked into the lowest rung of the minors and started getting hit! I thought, "How is this guy hitting me?" It never happened before!

Guess what? The guy who just bounced my best fastball into a Walla Walla onion field was the big guy on his high school or college team, too. Once you recognize you are not the best player on the field, you have to adjust and deal with it, and a lot of otherwise-talented guys just can't.

You have to start paying attention and working harder and listening to coaches and practicing in a way you never had to before. That's what "paying the price" means: digging more deeply into your competitive nature once you can't throw your glove on the field and win anymore.

You have to adjust your expectations, too. In the pros, you win .600 of the time long enough—and are in the Hall of Fame. You win .600 in high school or college—and don't even make All-League, let alone get drafted. As a pro you have to develop a tolerance for losing, going on to the next game, and competing. Not everybody wants to do this, or can.

Sometimes you hear people say, "The fans care more about winning than the players do." In a way, that's true. A player can't get all caught up in winning or losing one game, or sometimes even how successful a season is or is not. He's got to focus on staying healthy, being able to play through pain, and making adjustments. He's focusing on being *able* to compete, not the results of the competition. Sure he knows that losers don't last, but he can't afford to think about that—there's a game today.

So, it's almost the end of spring training and I'm still wearing a Rangers uniform and figuring I have a real shot at sticking, but can't be sure until the final roster is announced. In most cases, baseball is a strict meritocracy. It doesn't matter who your father is or where you went to school. Whether or not you can play matters. But one place baseball does grant privilege is the draft. How high you are drafted determines how much money you get and how many chances. A guy can hit a buck fifty, but if he was a high draft choice or became a millionaire the day he signed, he will get many more chances than a John Kruk, who got maybe $500 and a bus ticket.

Managers and the front office will look at a struggling high draft choice and say, "He must have potential or he wouldn't have been drafted that high." There are jobs on the line. A general manager can't have too many million-dollar bonus busts and keep working. Meanwhile, another team will take a chance on a failed high draft choice, hoping that the kid will figure it out on their watch. This can happen again and again.

If you didn't get much to sign, you better look good from day one, and you for damn sure don't want to get hurt. Nobody is going to carry a pitcher from the bottom of the draft while he comes back from Tommy John surgery.

That's why talented kids today have agents way *before* they sign: to jockey for high draft positions. That means not only more bonus money for them now, but also more time to make good later.

I was considered a decent prospect, but the year that I signed with San Diego, they also had the No. 3 pick in the draft, a pitcher from Dallas named Jimmy Jones. He eventually made the majors, but he didn't make a big splash. He didn't approach what a team hopes for from a top five pick, but that is not unusual. Take a look at history. Some No. 1's never make the show at all.

I signed for $18,000 and he got $102,000, so the way the Padres looked at us was a little different. They were going to do everything they could to move him along. He was going to get more chances. Eventually, the numbers on a bonus contract fade away and the numbers on a stat sheet take over, and again, it becomes all about performance. But the bigger the number on the bonus check, the longer it takes for them to fade.

Kruk's signing for peanuts worked against him, but so did the fact that he looked like the guy who mows your lawn. When you looked at him, even in his early days, you never thought he would have a major league career. He was a little overweight, even back then. He can't throw real well. He was an outfielder, and if you are a pitcher, you say to yourself, "Is this chubby guy going to run down anything in the gap for me?"

Then you look in the stat book and see he's hitting .340 with power. But what does the front office say? "Oh, yeah, he can hit down here, but wait until he gets to Double A." When he hits there, they say Triple A, then the majors. That is the big secret to *Moneyball,* the book that tells how the A's win games with no money. They scout numbers rather than bodies. They conclude that a guy like Kruk, who produces all along the way up to the majors, can probably perform in the big leagues, too. Likewise, a lot of guys who got big money because they *looked* like ballplayers turned out not to be. That's how guys like Chad Bradford and Jack Cust have had careers.

Casey Stengel used this same method to conclude that Yogi Berra ought to be a catcher. Berra looked like a yogi, short and squat. His language, as so famously documented, was a little confusing. People, including Yankees manger Bucky Harris, thought he wasn't smart enough or agile enough to catch. They thought the outfield was his future.

When Stengel took the Yankees' reins in 1949, he noticed that even though Yogi Berra didn't look like Joe DiMaggio, he did everything well. He hit, threw, and was even among the faster runners. He may have also noticed, had such statistics been available, that Berra was no more than an average outfielder. He brought in Hall of Fame catcher Bill Dickey to tutor Berra, and the rest is history. As an outfielder, the 25-to-30 homers Yogi hit every year would have been good but hardly unprecedented. As a catcher, it made him one of the all-time best. Judging players by performance rather than appearance is still considered revolutionary. Sixty years ago it was considered genius, and in a way, it was.

Of course, sometimes a player never gets a chance and you can't figure out exactly why. Rick Lancellotti was a first baseman for the Padres in Triple A forever, always hit well, and never got a chance. Some fans called him "The Home Run God of Buffalo." He hit 276 homers in the minor leagues, which earned him a total of 65 major league at-bats spread over eight years with three different teams.

Other guys get passed over for years but eventually break through. Marcus Thames hit a homer off Randy Johnson in his first major league at-bat, but he only got 13 of them with the Yankees. It looked like he would turn into the home run god of the Toledo Mud Hens had two events not transpired. When Tigers manager Alan Trammell sent him down in 2005 in order to keep all-but-finished outfielder Bobby Higginson, it caused dissension in the clubhouse, said to have been led by Dmitri Young. Coupled with a disappointing season, this cost the former star shortstop his managerial job.

His replacement, Jim Leyland, was encouraged to keep Thames with the big club partly through the recommendation of his brother, a Roman Catholic priest in Toledo. Thames has gone on to hit more home runs per times at-bat than just about anyone else in baseball.

You hear talk of Quadruple A players, and maybe there are guys who can consistently tear up the minors but can't compete in the majors, but I think most of them just never got the right chance with the right team. Either that or they just can't mentally survive under the big tent. Even a Hall of Famer like Tom Seaver says he was never the best pitcher on his team until he got to the majors. Until then, he performed just well enough to get to the next level.

My roommate Bobby Witt made the big-league roster about four days before the end of spring training, but I was still on the bubble. I just tried to prepare myself to go either way, to Triple A or Texas. After all, it's no big sin to get sent down. Mickey Mantle was sent down. You can pout, or you can go down and try to improve. If you get sent down, there are some flaws in your game that need to get better. You have to be philosophical about it, as hard as that is for a ballplayer.

Of course, I made the team that spring, but they didn't tell me until the last two days of spring training. Because of the control issues I'd had everywhere in the minors, and because I had not really faced prime competition until I went to Puerto Rico, I was a long shot. Fortunately for me, Bobby Valentine's hiring was part of a huge Rangers youth movement. He called me into his office and told me I'd made the club as a reliever. I was as excited as hell. I'm sure Bobby Witt and I celebrated pretty well. The fact that I don't remember exactly what we did probably confirms it.

The youth movement worked, at least for that year. We won 87 games, 25 more than in 1985. We finished second, five games behind the Angels. Steve Buechele at third and Oddibe McDowell in center had their first years as regulars. Pete Incaviglia and Ruben Sierra also made the team for the first time, Pete right out of college. Besides me, three of our starting pitchers were rookies: Witt, Ed Correa, and Jose Guzman. Tom House was mother hen to all the rookie pitchers.

I had been inside the Rangers locker room before, because I stayed there during the winter and worked out. But this was different. It was nice to walk in and see my own locker. There was no pecking order or seniority, no "mystic aura" because some locker used to belong to Babe Ruth or anything. It's not like we were in awe of where Jeff Burroughs had once changed his pants.

They gave me No. 28, which I wore for a long time, though I'm more known for wearing No. 99. They wouldn't give it to me for a long time in my career. I guess they were waiting until I became an important enough player. There was no deep reason for it. I was just a Mark Gastineau fan. He wore it as a New York Jets defensive end when he was sacking every quarterback in sight. You might say he played football the way I pitched, or at least the way I hoped to pitch.

I didn't have to wait long to get into a game. I pitched the ninth inning of our second game, a 3–1 loss to Doyle Alexander and the Blue Jays. I got my first strikeout, Lloyd Mosby, and gave up my first walk, Tony Fernandez, who was promptly thrown out trying to steal after I picked him off first base. I was a nervous wreck. You figure it they put you on the roster, they must know what they are doing, but you never know until you go out and do it. I got most of the butterflies out that first game. In my second game, and for all of them afterwards, I felt a lot better.

I led the league in games pitched with 80 and struck out almost a batter an inning. As usual, I gave up more walks than hits. I gave up my first homer toward the end of the month to Billy Jo Robidoux, a Brewers rookie who was regarded highly enough to have his own "Rated Rookie" baseball card, which I sure never had. The homer he hit off me contributed mightily to his season total of…one. He ended up batting .209 with only five homers for his career, but if he could have hit off me every day, he'd be in the Hall of Fame—3-for-3 lifetime. I still haven't gotten him out. It was ball night, we got killed 10–2, and I gave up four runs in less than two innings. When Billy Joe went deep to center, everybody threw the balls back on the field.

* * *

The Rangers did not have a tradition of hazing rookies. We didn't have to wear woman's clothes or polish anybody's cleats, or sing our high school fight songs. But there were a couple of rather interesting and creative pranks, most of which were fallen into by Pete Incaviglia.

Inky walked off the campus of Oklahoma State right into the big leagues. He did a great Jimmie Foxx imitation in college and was one of the biggest boppers in NCAA history. So when he made the team, he had no experience on a professional baseball field or in a clubhouse. He found his way around the field okay; the clubhouse was another matter.

Veterans are always looking to pull jokes on rookies, and soon they discovered that Pete was their most likely fall guy. If some vet

Pete Incaviglia was a savvy player on the diamond, but he often fell victim to pranks in the clubhouse. (AP Images)

tried to hook me, I'd just say, "Okay, fine," and go on my way. I'd beaten around the minor-league bushes enough to know what sick minds occupy baseball clubhouses. Not Inky.

I must admit, the teamwork necessary to pull the classic "Three Man Lift" on Pete was impressive. One day, Bobby Jones just says, to no one in particular, "Ya know, I bet I can lift those three guys this year."

And the other guys chime right in: "No way. I'll bet you a hundred dollars you can't do it."

And Jones replies, "No, really. I almost did it last year, and I've been working out."

"I'll bet a *thousand* you can't!" somebody else chirps.

Naturally Inky is curious. "What are you talking about?" he asks Jones.

"Ok, Ink, you're a big guy," Jones says. "You go pick any two guys in the clubhouse, and we'll lay you all down on the floor. You'll get all locked up. Then I will pick all three of you off the ground, up to my waist."

Pete says, "No way you can do that!" But the other guys are betting more and more money, and Jones is taking all the bets, and they all act like he almost did it last year. Of course, Incaviglia picks the two other biggest guys on the team, Larry Parrish and Gary Ward. They both went about 220 pounds, and Pete was about 240. They all got down on the floor and put Inky in the middle. They put his arms behind their heads, and then they lock legs and clamp down. As soon as Inky is completely immobilized, Jones says, "You ready?" And Inky says he is.

Then everybody goes and gets whatever they have that squirts: shampoo, liquid soap, after-shave lotion. Some guys find mayonnaise and ketchup. This is about five minutes before game time. Inky's in uniform, and he can't move. We cover him with everything we can think of.

Then the final touch: the spittoons. They contained a heady mixture of used tobacco juice and kitty litter. He just fell for everything that year. When they mention the adjustments of coming to the big leagues, they don't include the Three Man Lift, but they ought to.

* * *

There are a lot of things you run up against in the big leagues that are scarier than the Three Man Lift. Everybody needs a mentor, a kind of big brother, not so much to help you on the field as off it. Mine was Dickie Noles. That might surprise some people, because Dickie had been through it all, including drugs and alcohol. When we were in Texas, we used to go to high schools and talk to the kids. I was like one of the kids listening to his stories. He talked about all the things out there that can be your downfall. He warned about the people from different walks of life that do not have your best interests at heart. He always said, "Your life is not based on your dreams but the decisions that you make." He said that to me in 1985, and it has always stayed with me.

I hope I helped some of the younger guys along the way, too. Bobby Ayrault was only a couple of years younger than me when he came up in 1992. I suggested we live together, and I told him about what I went through in adjusting to the big leagues: what he would see and how to approach things. Not everything you tell somebody is going to be exactly right for them, but you hope they filter through it and take what is useful.

Teams have seminars now about what to expect and how to handle yourself. They didn't do that back when I played. We had people come in and tell us about drugs, alcohol, and gambling. They told us about the people who might approach you and what you should do, but it's a lot more in-depth now, which is good. Today, with the money that is out there, the vast variety of drugs, performance-enhancing and otherwise, and just the daily scrutiny that players endure, there are more distractions and potentially destructive diversions than ever.

The path to the big leagues is usually dusty and boring, and it's neither glamorous nor heroic. You get there through a combination of ability and focus, which you can control a little, and the ability to stay healthy and be in the right place at the right time, which you cannot control. That's why every player, especially after he retires and looks back on everything, knows that if he has had a big-league career of any duration, he's been one lucky man.

He's also learned how to make adjustments from year to year, game to game, pitch to pitch.

~

Chapter Two

On the Mound

Welcome to the major league pitching mound. Mounds differ a little from field to field, but not much. I didn't hate any of them, but the only one I didn't like was the one every other pitcher loved—the mound in Dodger Stadium. Everybody else liked it because it was high. I didn't like it for the same reason. I had a really long stride, and that mound didn't have enough slope for me. My front foot hit too soon.

I always threw from the left side of the rubber and hoped nobody made a big hole there. Usually it was fine, but if it wasn't, I was stuck with it. In the late innings, if somebody had already dug in for a hundred pitches or more, there was nothing I could do about it. If you saw the replay of Mark "The Bird" Fidrych on MLB television after he died on April 13, 2009, you saw him down on his hands and knees, playing with the dirt on the mound. He was repairing the holes that the other pitcher dug, though in a rather obsessive, unique manner. And he was doing his groundskeeping as a starter, repairing it one inning at a time. If he had been a closer, he would have needed a shovel.

I walked out there an average of 70 times a year from 1986–93. It might be one of the few places to work where the better you do,

My natural pitching motion carried me off of the mound. (AP Images)

the less time you spend there. A closer might spend a day or two waiting to throw a dozen pitches. Out of that dozen, the game will turn on only one or two.

That's why I was successful as a closer. It fit my personality— get in there, get it done, and get out. Out of all the things that a major-league ballplayer has to do, the one thing I got exactly right was that I never wanted a day off. I always took the baseball. I figured if I could pull my pants on, I could pitch. Managers appreciated this then, and they would today if the game was still sensible about using pitchers.

Underusing a pitcher is terrible, way worse than overusing a guy, because pitching is how you build arm strength. The more I threw, the better I threw. One stretch in Texas in August 1986, when Dale Mohorcic got some headlines for pitching in 13 straight games, I pitched in nine of them. A few years later, I won Pitcher of the Month for August 1991. I threw 22 innings in 15 games as a closer, allowed 10 hits, struck out 22, walked 16, saved five, and went 8–1. I threw my best when I pitched in game after game after game.

A guy will suffer more from *not* pitching three or four days in a row than he will from pitching that many games, but most managers don't believe that anymore, from what I see. The Red Sox lost a game in early June 2009 when they didn't use Jonathan Papelbon because he was "not available." He had thrown two games in a row. I'm like, "Are they *kidding*? Two whole days in a row!"

Overworking is more of a mental thing than it is a physical condition. A pitcher needs as much mental conditioning as he does physical. You get taken out after 100 pitches no matter what the situation, you begin to think you can't throw pitch No. 101. You only pitch a guy one inning at a time, and he begins to think that's all he can throw. Yes, there is something to having your pitchers know their roles, but it gets overdone today: this guy only pitches the seventh, that guy only pitches the ninth. Another guy only faces lefties. It's gotten so that Yankees fans get nervous if Mariano Rivera is asked to pitch more than one inning. Fortunately for them, it doesn't seem to make Mariano nervous.

If you can't throw more than one inning, there's something really wrong.

I could pitch every day, as much as they wanted me to. I never went to the park and said, "I can't throw today." I think that's why my arm stayed strong. Of course, I didn't blow out my elbow by throwing a lot of sliders, or mess up my shoulder with curves. I threw every day, even if I didn't get in the game, either long toss or off a mound. That's unusual today, but it didn't used to be. I think the majority of arm injuries are caused because pitchers don't throw enough.

The pitch count is the most overblown waste of time in baseball. In 1952, Robin Roberts started 37 games and completed 30. Mickey Lolich averaged more than 300 innings a year for seven years from 1969–75. Okay, maybe those guys were exceptions. Not many pitchers were doing that, even in their day. But who are the exceptions today? Aren't baseball players supposed to be bigger and stronger? Why is it that big, strong hitters like Albert Pujols and Ryan Howard are putting up numbers that stand with any era in baseball, while in the National League in 2008, only 18 pitchers logged as many as 200 innings? That's just about one per team. Are you telling me there are exactly zero pitchers in the National League who can come within a hundred innings of Mickey Lolich's highest total! He wasn't Cy Young.

I've never understood the idea behind pitch counts. I threw more than 150 pitches in starts in the minors. I once threw more than 200 pitches in a seven-inning game in high school! It's all about the mind. If you train your arm to throw, it can throw. A marathon runner can't train by running sprints. But if you are only training your arm to throw 100 pitches, that's where it's going to stop. You have guys who are 6'4" 250 pounds out there looking to the bullpen in the sixth inning because they know they are at 90 pitches. They think they're done because they know the manager and the pitching coach won't let them be anything else.

Years ago, the term "seven-inning pitcher" was an insult. Now it's a compliment. One of the guys who used to be slammed because he couldn't finish games was Milt Pappas, who is remembered today mostly for being traded from Baltimore for Frank Robinson. He came up with the Orioles in 1957 at age 18 and was taking a regular turn at 19. His manager, Paul Richards, might be the first big-league manager who was conscious of not blowing out the arms of young pitchers. In 1960, he had five starters who were either 21 or 22, including Pappas. Richards carefully protected their arms against overuse.

Hall of Fame broadcaster Ernie Harwell, who was doing the Orioles' games then, remembered Richards using pitch counts with Pappas and others. It didn't do much good. Chuck Estrada and Jerry Walker were basically finished at 25, and Steve Barber's career was sore-armed into mediocrity. Only Pappas and Jack Fisher lasted, and neither fulfilled their early promise.

More typical were the Tigers of that same era, who were burning through the young arms of Frank Lary, Billy Hoeft, Jim Bunning, and Paul Foytack as fast as they could. Lary, Hoeft, and Foytack only had a few good years, but Bunning lasted forever and went into the Hall of Fame. And it was Bunning who threw like he would dislocate several joints with every pitch he tossed! Each of his appendages seemed to go in a different direction. Frankly, his finishing motion was a little like mine.

It doesn't seem to me that it makes a lot of difference whether you baby an arm or not. Pitching is an unnatural act. It's likely to hurt your arm. Are there any fewer arm injuries today because of pitch counts? It seems to me there are more.

Paul Richards is also said to be the first manager to go to a five-man starting rotation back when he had those five really young pitchers, though it took many years for all the teams to switch from four starters to five. I still don't know why they did.

It made sense for Richards. He was trying not to burn out kids. But let's look at the facts. One, it didn't succeed, as the "Baby Birds" never did fly very high or very long. Two, it makes no sense at all today.

How many teams use five-man rotations? All of them. How many teams have five decent starters? None of them. What's wrong with this picture? Why give as many starts to a guy who ought to be in Triple A as you give to your ace? Take the 30 starts your fifth

Tigers pitcher Jim Bunning in 1962. (AP Images)

starter is getting and distribute them to your other four. So if a
starter makes every turn, he would get 35–37 starts instead of 31
or 32 and pitch another 50–60 innings. Would you rather see guys
like C.C. Sabathia and Roy Oswalt pitch another 50 innings, or see
20 percent of major-league games used as tryouts for whatever
Triple A pitcher might survive into the fifth inning? Which strategy gives your team a better chance to win?

Will your top four starters be worse throwing 250 innings rather than 210? Maybe a little, but it's not like they will turn into Jose Lima for those extra starts, either. It might even make them stronger when they need to be.

There is some evidence that starters who rack up big innings more than two years in a row are at a bigger risk for injury. Yes, now. I'm thinking that is because pitchers are not conditioned mentally or physically to throw nearly as much as they can.

Again, a five-man rotation is meant to save arms. But it doesn't. Good mechanics saves arms. Someday a manager is going to win a pennant by having the guts to go to a four-man rotation with the support of his front office. He will be proclaimed a courageous genius, and soon everybody will be back to four. It could happen in Texas.

I love what Nolan Ryan is doing with the Rangers. He's having his guys throw batting practice and long toss, like pitchers used to. He's having them throw between starts. Look at Kevin Millwood. Suddenly he's throwing the most innings per start of anybody in the majors! It helps his team by saving its pen and having a front-line starter compete longer at higher efficiency. The Rangers can't win by bludgeoning the other team. They tried that. They have to pitch. They are pitching better in 2009 and winning more. The human body is an amazing thing. It can do what you ask it to do if you do it in the right way.

The Cubs and their manager, Dusty Baker, caught a lot of flack a few years ago because Kerry Wood and Mark Prior both got hurt. Their injuries had nothing to do with too many pitches. They had to do with horrible mechanics. Prior was said to have great mechanics? Wrong. Neither pitcher ever got to their back side. That falls squarely on the pitching coach. It comes from worrying about working from a slide step, being quick to the plate. You hear that all the time, "Be quick to the plate." It's more important to throw a quality pitch with good mechanics.

These guys never got to their back sides during their windups. If your kick leg at some point in your motion does not get even with your post leg, you are rushing. "Rushing" means that your arm is lagging behind your body and you have to muscle the ball to get it there with anything on it.

Both Wood and Prior threw with their kick legs way out in front. They were already starting down the mound before their arms had reached the release point. There is no telling how long those guys could have pitched if someone had just taken them aside and said, "Get to your post leg!" Neither one of them ever did. The slide step probably helped murder both those arms.

It is the exact same thing as when a hitter is fooled by an off-speed pitch and lunges forward. He's lost all the power in his legs and is just swinging with his arms. He is *not* going to hit that pitch very far. A pitcher who doesn't get to his back side is throwing just with his arm. He's lost the power of his legs, chest, shoulders, everything. It's not how many pitches you throw; it's the mechanics you use to throw them.

One thing that is a must in helping a pitcher's mechanics and stamina is running—either between starts or, if you are a reliever, just about every day. There has always been some disagreement about how *much* pitchers should run. Johnny Sain, who was a genius pitching coach in the 1960s, didn't believe in running at all. He thought a pitcher got stronger by pitching. Fine. The point is not *how* a pitcher's legs get strong but that they do. Today, a lot of pitchers are in the workout rooms on the bikes. That works.

Starters who can go deep into games are the ones who can keep their legs under them. If you hear a coach say, "He started to lose his legs," it means his legs start to collapse, to buckle at the end of a pitch. That shoots him down the mound, which means he is leaving pitches up because his arm can't catch up to his body. He begins to "sit on his back side," meaning he's trying to drop and drive instead of standing tall and falling. He's trying to generate with his body what ought to be done by gravity. He can't do it. Get him out.

Another thing—today, when a young pitcher comes up to the majors as a starter, they often limit the number of innings he can throw all year. The Yankees treated Joba Chamberlain in 2008 like his arm was made of glass. He started out in the bullpen and then made only 12 starts, reaching the seventh inning only once. And what happened? He still got hurt! He made his last start August 4 and went on the disabled list with rotator cuff tendinitis. He pitched 11 innings the rest of the season.

How soon a young pitcher can work up to more innings depends on the guy holding the ball. If you are ready to work hard and train your body to do it, your body will do it. Could Joba have thrown more? Who knows? He wasn't given the chance. But we do know that limiting his pitch counts and innings did not save him from injury, which was the whole point of doing it. And it might have implanted in his mind that his arm is fragile, which surely is not going to help him gut it out in a close game. He won't be able to find something more because he's never been asked to look for more.

It's still a big topic in New York whether Joba should start or relieve. Well, you don't have to make a decision now that has to last forever. Everybody acts like it, but it should not be that tough to go from starting to relieving and back again. You don't want to do it back and forth within the same season too much, but from year to year, that would be fine. John Smoltz did it, and he was battling a series of arm miseries. The difference is more in mental preparation than physical strain.

People may say I'm wrong, but just because Joba Chamberlain has four good pitches does not mean the Yankees are a better team with him starting. Hands down, they would be better with him throwing the seventh and eighth inning. You will never convince me otherwise.

Now, if the Yankees get somebody with stuff as dominating as Joba has that they can use as a setup guy, fine, start Joba. But as of now, he would be more valuable as a shut-down setup man than as a slightly better-than-average No. 3 or No. 4 starter who has trouble getting out of the sixth inning.

You take a kid like Joba, yes, he has four pitches. But when you watch him start, after one trip through the lineup, he has to use brain power and start thinking. You can see his temperament and personality on the mound. He's a wound-up guy, high strung. He's gotten some criticism for showing too much emotion when he gets a big strikeout. That reminds me of when Bobby Valentine sent me to a hypnotist to calm me down. I did not want to calm down. Neither does Joba. That's who we are, and he ought to be used in a position where his temperament is a positive not a negative. That would be the late innings, not starting. We can't all be stoic, John Wayne–types like Catfish Hunter or Fergie Jenkins. You couldn't tell from the expression on those guys' faces whether the hitter just struck out or homered.

Joba is perfectly constructed for the bullpen. He reminds me of me. My temperament was not suited to starting *at all*. I was all, "Give me the damned ball!" Let that adrenaline go to work.

So what did the Yankees do? They put Phil Hughes in the pen! He's doing okay, but anyone can see that Phil has a starter's personality. He can't do in the seventh and eighth what Joba can do, but he *can* do what Joba can do as a starter. If you have a guy with Phil Hughes' stuff that can't be your fourth or fifth starter now, get rid of him.

The argument at the beginning of 2009 was, "Would you put a young Roger Clemens in the bullpen?" Well, no, but just as Lloyd

Bentsen once famously reminded Dan Quayle that Quayle was no Jack Kennedy, Joba Chamberlain is no Roger Clemens. Not in 2009, at least.

The White Sox made Goose Gossage a starter for one year. He came up at age 20 and had four years as a reliever. In 1975, he led the league in saves. For this, he was "rewarded" by being turned into a starter. He went 9–17.

Okay, the 1976 White Sox were terrible, and Carl Hubbell would have struggled to be .500 with them, but still. He just wasn't that great as a starter. Most telling was his strikeout rate, which was 8.3 per nine innings as a reliever and only 5.4 as a starter.

When you get to the fifth inning, it is not about throwing, it is about pitching. Goose could dominate throwing his fastball for one or two innings. When he tried to throw it for six or seven, however, it became very hittable. You see a guy one time, and you can dominate him with your one great pitch. You see him two or three times, hitters will adjust. He has to use other pitches. That's why Mariano Rivera was moved to the bullpen in the first place. He failed as a starter because all he had was one great pitch. He set up games for John Wetteland in 1996. Wetteland also began as a starter but was switched to the pen by the Dodgers.

Joba has the pitches, but as of 2009, he does not know how to use them. Maybe he will learn and maybe he won't, but it makes as much sense to use Joba Chamberlain as a starter as it does to start Mariano Rivera. The Yankees could use Joba as a reliever in 2010 and try him as a starter again the next year. It will *not* hurt the guy to pitch!

It's all about mechanics. If you have solid mechanics, you can throw all day long. When a starter gets tired and his mechanics start to fade, when he's dropping his arm and not getting to his back side, *that's* the time to get him out. Teams are risking injury

Joba Chamberlain pitched against the Red Sox at Yankee Stadium on September 25, 2009.

at that point, but it requires a pitching coach and a manager to make a judgment. A pitch count requires no judgment.

Even worse than relying on pitch counts as a guide to how a pitcher ought to be used is using the radar gun. If I were a pitching coach, I'd lobby hard to get the guns turned off in the stadiums. You absolutely have pitchers who look at that scoreboard to see how hard they are throwing. Brett Myers looked up so much they quit putting the velocity up there when he pitched.

I never cared what the guns said. If you can't tell whether or not you have good velocity, there is something wrong. Those radar guns are so far off it's not funny. They give readings way too high, trust me. It's a lazy way for broadcasters to "report" how a pitcher is doing. You will see graphics that give the high and low velocity a starter has reached. That might be interesting, assuming the numbers were anywhere close to reality, but it tells absolutely nothing about how well a pitcher is doing. How many times you hear, "Wow! That pitch was 98 mph!" Of course, the batter hit it into the upper deck....

I'm sure this all comes from drafting a potential pitching ace and sending him to the minors. You don't want him throwing 150 pitches in Class A so some minor-league manager can beat Lakeland 1–0 in 12 innings, and the organization makes a rule: limit this guy to 70 pitches, or whatever. The trouble is, this now continues all the way to the majors, and managers continue this mindless approach to pitching.

Nobody will blame you if your young pitcher gets hurt if he never threw more than 120 pitches in a game. You have covered your ass. Nobody blamed Joe Girardi for Chamberlain's injury because he followed the "rules." But someone in the organization might consider that they took what was widely considered the best young arm in baseball and found a way to throw it only 100 innings, or 13 fewer than Darrell Rasner threw for them, a pitcher who, if you look up "replacement level starter" in the dictionary, you'll find a picture of his baseball card. And Joba's great arm still got hurt!

Daisuke "Dice-K" Matsuzaka is another pitcher I think suffers in a different way from pitch counts. In 2008, he never threw more than 118 pitches in any of his 29 starts. He averaged fewer than six innings per start. Anybody who watches him knows that he throws a lot of pitches per inning. That's his style; always has been. But all the experts said, "He might be able to get away with that in Japan, but not here." He couldn't get away with it because the Red Sox wouldn't let him.

Matsuzaka was taken out of eight starts in 2008 before he had given up a run. Eight! Matsuzaka does it right. The Japanese are way ahead of us when it comes to pitching mechanics. You watch just about every Japanese pitcher who comes to the big leagues. They do what I call "stand tall and fall."

They allow themselves to gather. By that I mean they bring their hands together and find a center of gravity where they can use their core strength. You very seldom see a Japanese pitcher rushing down the mound. You can see Dice-K literally picking up speed as he lets gravity take his body down and forward. You gather yourself, then stand tall and fall. If your legs are weak, I don't mean physically weak, but if your legs are collapsing on your back side, then you have effectively lowered the mound. Now you are throwing uphill.

There is no such thing as a "drop and drive" pitcher. Maybe Tom Seaver was the only one, but if you watch him, once he dropped down, he never came back up. Maybe he didn't "stand tall," but he sure as hell fell. He didn't stand as high, so he fell lower. He fell so low, you could see the dirt on his right knee. In fact, it came to be known as "the Seaver spot." It was a soiled spot about the size of a quarter. If you didn't see it in the first inning, you might have a chance to get to him early, because it meant he had not gotten his delivery where it needed to be during his warmups. Once you saw that spot, he was hard to beat.

It's like in the movie *Gladiator* when they used catapults to shoot those big balls of fire. If they made the base of those things out of rubber, they wouldn't shoot anything. The base has to be strong. Your back side has to be strong, or else your pitch is going straight into the dirt. If you see a wild pitch, a *really* wild pitch, one that hits the dirt about two feet in front of the plate, it was probably created not from a poor motion by the arm but by a weak post leg right from the beginning of the delivery.

If people paid attention to mechanics, there would be fewer sore arms and no need for pitch counts. Without watching the mechanics, or understanding what you are seeing, you can count all you want and there will still be sore arms. That's baseball today.

When Tom House was our pitching coach at Texas, he was all about mechanics. He always believed in me. Without Tom, maybe I get to the majors, maybe I don't. The Rangers' pitching staff when I was rookie in 1986 was filled with young guys throwing in the 90s. We might not know where it was going, but it would get there in a hurry.

Arm problems soon plagued a lot of those young pitchers. Ed Correa had arm problems forever—before, after, and during the times he was pitching well. Jose Guzman started regularly for six years but was finished at 31. I was 32 when I packed it in. Bobby Witt lasted a long time, but he always walked more guys than a starter can afford and finished under .500.

House was responsible for getting those kids to the majors and keeping us there. He tried to simplify our motion, get all the parts going in the same direction. He was a huge help to me, taking away all the extraneous movements. That was more than 20 years ago, and now every pitching coach does it.

If you look back through baseball history, the further back you go, the bigger and more elaborate the windups, the leg kicks, and the motions were. It seemed like it took Bob Feller about 10 minutes to throw a pitch. Warren Spahn and Juan Marichal's leg kicks seem impossible, unless you've seen Dontrelle Willis or Orlando Hernandez. Except for Paul Byrd, who pitches like he stepped out of a black-and-white film of the St. Louis Browns, the trend is toward "less is more." The less motion, the more success.

Don Larsen might have started this when he pitched his perfect game in the 1956 World Series. He had just gone to a "no windup" motion to improve his control and keep his focus, and the Brooklyn Dodgers, who had not seen it before, spent the whole game behind his pitches. His teammate Bob Turley started using it, too, and two years later he won the Cy Young Award and it was his turn to be World Series hero.

Yet neither of these guys had great or sustained success. Larsen was in and out of Casey Stengel's rotation and finished as a reliever in the National League. Turley broke down right after his big year and never recovered.

I'm not sure what Tom could have done to avoid these sore arms or really improve our control past a certain point. If any pitching coach comes up with the cure for sore arms, he will immediately be escorted to the Hall of Fame. It's about as likely to happen as a cure for stupid.

A coach can only do so much to refine a pitcher's motion, and then it is up to the pitcher to be able to repeat it again and again and again. Control is all from the neck up. A lot of times you talk yourself out of throwing strikes. A lot of it depends on the situation. If I came into a game with a guy at the plate I know can hit me, and the next guy not so much, then I'm not going to give this guy anything good to hit. He's either going to swing at bad balls, or I'm going to walk him.

Bobby Valentine hired Tom House as pitching coach, so he certainly appreciated the mental aspect of pitching, even if some of House's ideas seemed a little weird to me. That's why he sent me to a hypnotist. Bobby wanted me to control my emotions better on the mound. And it worked! I did it. I could literally go out there and give up a home run and not care at all. I hated it.

I told him, "Look. I pitch on emotion. I don't want to go out there emotionless. I want to control my emotions enough to make them work for me. I can't go out there and be a zombie."

There is definitely a special mentality to being a closer, just like there is to starting or middle relief. Todd Jones was a setup guy with great stuff when I played with him. He was young and hadn't learned a lot about the game. As he got older, eventually his stuff wasn't as great, but he learned how to pitch. He finished with 319 saves. Only a handful of guys have more. He was unusual as a closer, because he threw three or four pitches. None were dominant, but he threw strikes. He gave up hits but kept the ball in the ballpark. Most closers have one great pitch and it's just, "Here it is. Try to hit it."

It was his make-up more than his stuff that made him a closer. Nothing seemed to bother him. He had a cool, placid demeanor. It seems like closers come in two varieties: hot and cool. I was hot, very intense, like Goose. We ran on adrenaline. So did Al Hrabosky. Now Joel Zumaya, Todd Jones' bullpen mate for a couple of years in Detroit, does. Joba Chamberlain, as I said, has the stuff to start but the adrenaline to close.

Rob Dibble was another guy who wore his emotions on his sleeve. If Dibble was upset, everybody in the ballpark knew it. I could relate to that. I loved watching him.

I thought I let it all hang out with every pitch, but he was even more demonstrative than I was! Everybody talked about his fast-ball, but it was his filthy slider that made him so great. I thought he would be a guy who came into the league in a blaze of glory, and he went out the same way shortly thereafter because there no way he was going to hold up mechanically with that motion. He was finished at 31.

He was one of the very few pitchers that made me look sane.

Others guy like Todd, Lee Smith, and Bruce Sutter are from the relaxed school of closing. Dennis Eckersley, too. Mariano Rivera seems almost meditative. If you had his cutter, why would you *not* be relaxed?

I needed to be wide open and intense. Others had to be relaxed. The idea is to get to that place where nothing bothers you; nothing distracts you; nothing intimidates you. You have to get to that one place where you can compete. It doesn't matter how you get there.

I more or less *had* to be a closer, because if you'd pitch me in the fifth, sixth, or seventh innings, I would not have gotten people out. In the middle innings of a game, the hitters are more selective. But if you put a guy at the plate in the ninth inning with the game on the line and get ahead of him with strike one, you don't have to throw him another strike. That's what a lot of pitchers don't understand. Goose Gossage told me one time, and I've never forgotten it, "Too much control in a closer is dangerous."

If you pound that strike zone in the ninth inning...strikes are hittable. There is no question about it. If you throw nothing but strikes, you are going to get pounded. But with the game on the line and that hitter's ego on the line, every hitter wants to get up tomorrow morning and read the headline that his homer won the game. A pitcher can take advantage of that. Get ahead of him with strike one, then make him swing at pitches that are not strikes.

I did *not* get people out by throwing strikes. I got outs by people swinging at balls. If you can't put a hitter on the defensive by throwing strike one, though, it gets tough on you. But as soon as you get them in the hole, you can expand that strike zone as much as you want.

Sure, some great relievers like Dennis Eckersley and Mariano Rivera are known for having great control. But that can cost you, too. The pitch Eck threw to Kirk Gibson that he hit for that famous homer in the 1988 World Series was a strike. In fact, it was a helluva pitch, a backdoor slider on the outside corner. The only problem was that Gibson, with two bad knees, didn't have his usual bat speed and had been sitting on the bench for three hours hoping Eckersley would throw him a slider. If that pitch had been 3 inches outside, Gibson most likely strikes out and nobody ever gets to see the video—the one that every baseball fan has seen about a million times—of him pumping his arms while circling the bases. At worst, he's only on first with a walk.

Rivera, clearly among the greatest closers ever, lost a World Series by giving up three hits to Arizona hitters in the ninth inning in 2001. I'm guessing that Mark Grace, Tony Womack, and Luis Gonzalez all hit strikes because that's just about all Rivera throws. And my point is, you don't *have* to throw strikes to get Tony Womack out, not in the ninth inning and for sure not in the ninth inning of the World Series.

Needless to say, I threw Joe Carter one more strike that I should have in the 1993 Series.

You can't be too fine when you are closing. It works against you. Successful closing is all mentality. When you walk through the outfield fence, everybody in the ballpark—your team, the other team, the umpires, the fans, the hot dog vendors—should all know that game is over. If you take that mound as a closer and there is any doubt about your coming in, you are *not* ready to be a closer. It's not just how you think about yourself but the mentality of the fans and all the players, too. At a home game, there ought to be a big cheer. Closers feed off that kind of fan enthusiasm. Pitchers can feel it when it's not there, too.

When I came in to close, nobody wanted to face me. They didn't know whether they would get hit or not. That was part of it. They knew they were not going to get comfortable at-bats.

I had 91 minor-league appearances, and 90 of them were starts. I honestly hated starting from the minute I got into professional baseball—too much time between appearances. When you take a kid out of high school, he's usually pretty hyped up when he gets into a game. The issue with kid pitchers isn't so much the number of innings they throw but the number of times they have to deal with the adrenaline rush caused by the game itself. Going to the mound and having to deal with just the stress of pitching takes getting used to. Kids would get more out of going longer in fewer games, at least until they got used to the pump that comes with professional pitching.

They started throwing me out of the bullpen when I went to winter ball after the 1985 season. I went to big-league camp that spring. I threw 18 innings, gave up two runs, and made the team as a reliever. It's just one of those things. My personality was way more suited to coming out of the bullpen late than to starting one game and sitting around for four days.

Sometimes there are disagreements. Former Mets pitcher Aaron Heilman has a great arm and has usually been a pretty good reliever. But you always hear that he wants to start, and the Mets wouldn't let him. In 2007, when they lost the NL East by one game, they gave six starts to Brian Lawrence and two to Jason Vargas. They went 1–3 with a collective earned run average of 8.24. But zero starts for Aaron Heilman. I can understand why.

Whoever got him with his arm slot where it is should be pummeled. This is a big guy with a great arm. If he just stood tall and threw the ball downhill, he'd have a lot more success. But with his sidearm motion, his ball never changes planes. I don't care how hard you throw—and this kid throws hard—trust me, when he comes in the game, every left-handed hitter on the other team can't wait to step in the batter's box.

Heilman's splits against lefties started out okay, but they have been going south for a long time. In 2008, left-handed hitters had an on-base percentage of .425 and a slugging average of .567. You know who else did? Lance Berkman! You make every lefty who comes out of the dugout into Lance Berkman, and buddy, you are not going to start. If you want to beat Heilman as a starter, just load your lineup with lefties. He can't get 'em out. That's why the Mets started a guy not named Heilman in 162 games.

But if you got Heilman to throw over the top or even three-quarters to where he threw downhill and had some downward movement on his pitches, then you'd have something. Why didn't the Mets know this? Who knows? Maybe they did and they just

Goose Gossage was the closer in Chicago when I got traded there in 1989. I was traded to the Phillies in 1991.

could not get him to make the adjustments. I hated starting. Maybe Aaron hates throwing any way but the way he does. Sometimes you just have to accept what guys can do and not try to make them into what they are not. But if he can't adjust, he can't expect to start. His 2009 record against lefties has been a lot better, but he's still in the pen for the Cubs.

The only hero I ever had in baseball was Goose Gossage, so I guess it's not surprising I became a closer. He was a closer when being a closer didn't mean just pitching one inning or getting a save by getting the final out in the ninth. When he came to the Yankees and they won it all in 1978, he pitched 134 innings in 63 games. He *averaged* more than two innings per appearance. Twice in extra inning games he went seven!

Funny the way things go in baseball. Goose was the closer on the Cubs when I got traded there in 1989. We were in spring training together, he got released, and I took his job. It was really strange to take my hero's job. The thing about it is, you could not meet a better guy than Goose Gossage. He was absolutely wonderful to me. I'll never have anything but good things to say about him. It was an honor just to go to spring training with him. He was an example to me my whole career. I just loved how he approached the game. He threw as hard as he could every pitch. And that's how I approached it.

* * *

I threw a fastball and a slider. I never mastered an off-speed pitch. It just didn't go along with the way I thought. Now, looking back on it, I wish I had taken the time and worked harder to get a decent change of pace. A lot of different kinds of pitches have been called sliders over the years. Back in the 1920s, there was a pitch they called "a nickel curve" that was later called a slider. Burleigh

Grimes may not have invented it, but he was certainly among the first to use it.

"You start out thinking fastball," Hall of Famer Grimes said in an interview a few years before he died in 1985 at age 92. "Then at the last minute you think curve and turn the ball over. It comes in like a fastball but breaks a little bit right at the end."

What pitchers discovered by throwing sliders this way is that it puts a lot of stress on the elbow. If you try to break off a slider at the end to get just a little more bite, then you are asking for trouble. Just let it go and let your grip create the break.

Today the closest thing to that old-time nickel curve would be a knuckle curve, like Mike Mussina threw. You dig your index finger into the seam of the ball, which brings the knuckle up. That enables you to get a little more late movement. But that is a very rare pitch, and it's more of an off-speed pitch. Because it is off speed, it doesn't croak your elbow. Today a slider is a power pitch, and a lot of pitchers throw some variation of it.

Now it is a small, late-breaking pitch that you throw with the same motion as a fastball. The difference is all in the grip. For a fastball, you want your fingers on top of the ball and down through the middle. The slider grip is off center to the outside. You put more pressure on your middle finger and finish by cutting it off, like your middle finger is cutting through the ball but off center. It breaks down and in to a right-handed batter when thrown by a lefty like me.

If that sounds like a cutter, or cut fastball, that's because it is. It just depends on how much movement a pitcher gets. A little movement like Mariano Rivera's and it is called a cutter. It moves a couple of inches way late and breaks bats.

A bigger break like Brad Lidge produces and it's called a slider. It sort of disappears to the batter. He swings where he thinks it will be and gets air. Greg Maddux seemed to calibrate the break on his slider/cutter down to the millimeter, getting bigger or smaller breaks depending on what would put the hitter back in the dugout faster.

You could see Maddux was going to be tremendous even though he struggled his first year as a starter. He had guts like no one I've ever seen. He would throw inside to anyone. He did not care who it was. He is a very deceptive guy out on the mound. He weighed 175 pounds, maybe. Yeah, he had a bad body. If he ever used steroids, he ought to ask for a refund. What people don't realize is that he is just an awesome athlete. Really. He could go out and play basketball with anybody. Go out on a golf course and shoot 68. Baseball was not a hard game for him. How many guys can say that?

Only seven pitchers in history won more games than Greg's 355, and among them, only Warren Spahn pitched after 1929. The conventional wisdom was that after the five-man rotation became common somewhere back in the 1970s, the 300-game winner would become extinct since even aces would get fewer starts each year. Also, with starters going fewer innings every year, more decisions were going to the bullpen.

The conventional wisdom didn't count on pitchers staying around forever, allowing Roger Clemens, Greg Maddux, Randy Johnson, and Tom Glavine also to win 300, joining Seaver, Ryan, Sutton, Niekro, and Gaylord Perry, all who pitched recently enough to have battled Astroturf and designated hitters.

Maddux once said the secret of pitching is to throw balls when hitters are swinging and throw strikes when they are taking. That's a good philosophy, *if* you can read minds. Maybe Greg could. Maybe *that* was his secret.

The grip makes all the difference on a sinker, a slider, or any pitch. I threw nothing but four-seam fastballs my whole career. I never threw a two-seamer, which can have more movement but which can be "read" by the hitter sooner. It is a little easier for the hitter to pick up. I wanted late movement, where the ball seems to hop. I know a "rising fastball" is an optical illusion and a physical impossibility, but I got a lot of strikeouts on that illusion.

Some guys have fastballs that move and others just don't. It has a lot to do with the grip and release, but it really is just how a guy naturally throws the ball. Jack Morris said when he was throwing hard, he just threw right down the middle. His fastball would move somewhere and hit a corner. He didn't always know *which* corner.

Matt Lindstrom of the Marlins throws extremely hard and extremely straight. His fastball doesn't have a finish. When you are a power pitcher, you want to throw the ball on a downhill plane. That's when you hear "this guy's ball explodes." If you can get late movement, the ball comes in higher than the batter is calculating.

Kyle Farnsworth is a guy who got labeled as having a straight fastball. Commentators figure that must be the reason he has such an unfortunate propensity for giving up late-inning dingers. It is not that. He has a dominating fastball and doesn't use it. He throws way too many breaking balls and gets beat with them. If I were his pitching coach, I would work solely on locating his fastball. The best pitch in baseball is still a well-located fastball, because it gives the hitter the least time to react.

Sometimes pitchers look for a little more movement from sources other than their grip. Our friend Mr. Grimes was also the last pitcher legally to throw a spitball—in 1934, the year he retired. Who threw a spitball and when and at whom used to be a big topic of baseball conversation, but it isn't much anymore. This might be because of the split finger, which breaks down like a spitter and gives a pitcher the movement without the moisture, almost.

Wet your first two fingers, and be sure not to have them touch a seam on the baseball. Then you just throw it like a fastball. When you don't have a seam, it takes a lot of the rotation off the ball, which makes it drop. A spitter is a fastball where the bottom drops out. It is a lot faster than a splitter, which is its advantage.

Grimes said, "You squeeze out a spitter between your fingers and your thumb like you are squeezing out a wet watermelon seed." He's exactly right. You want a spitter to slip out of your hand with as little rotation as possible.

There is also such a thing as a "dry spitter." You don't put your thumb or any fingers on a seam. It slides off your fingers with little rotation, rather than rotating back like a fastball. It won't give you as much break as a wet one, but it can be a decent pitch and give you some downward movement.

There are still some spitballers around. You can tell when somebody says, "He's throwing it so hard, not losing any velocity from his fastball, but he's getting tremendous sink on the ball." Without casting any aspersions, the closest thing to a spitter was when Chien-Ming Wang was throwing what everybody called "his 95-mph sinker."

He's recently struggled to find that great pitch. Some people think he may have hurt his arm. I think he just needs to get on top of the ball again. I'm sure that is what he is trying to do. When a sinkerballer gets his fingers around the side of the ball rather than on top, he gets movement, but it's not real useful movement. It may run in or out, but it won't sink. If it doesn't change planes, you can't ever get out of the way of the barrel of the bat.

Of course, an injury might be the reason that Wang has trouble getting on top. He may have shoulder pain or stiffness that prevents it. A bad knee could do it, too.

Back in the day, spitters were more like UFOs: there were a lot more rumors than actual sightings. Even Gaylord Perry used it mostly for mind games. The various sleight-of-hand wiggles and wipes he went through were more to play with hitters' heads than their swings.

I think what used to be more prevalent was scratching or otherwise defacing a ball. If you can throw at major-league speed, even a little smudge or gouge can make a ball dance. That's why umps are forever throwing balls out after one or two pitches. There are many accounts of Whitey Ford using a sharp part of his wedding ring to cut balls. I always wondered how his wife felt about his filing down his ring. His catcher, Elston Howard, would also cut the ball with a sharp edge on his shin guard.

Former Orioles and Yankees catcher Elrod Hendricks wasn't overly huge for a big-league backstop, but his hands were big as shovels and just as hard. He could cut the seam of a ball using only his thumbnail.

Technology has all but eliminated this kind of chicanery—too many cameras. All those cameras actually created controversy when there didn't need to be any in the 2006 World Series. It was a big deal that Kenny Rogers had pine tar on the lower section of his pitching hand. It was a big deal to the media. It was *not* to anybody who had ever played. When it is cold, you cannot grip the baseball. Pine tar does nothing to change the rotation of the ball. It's not like Vaseline. It's just for feel. Hitters get to use pine tar all over their bats even though they are wearing batting gloves to improve their grip.

That's why the umpires didn't do anything about it and why Tony La Russa could not have cared less. Hey, if you are going to play the World Series in winter weather, you have to allow players to do something so they can play the damned game. If you are a hitter and complain because a pitcher wants to grip the ball, you are just looking for a reason to whine. If he's out there cutting or wetting it, however, that's another story.

As far as umps go, there are still pitcher's umps and hitter's umps, even though there have been efforts to make the strike zone more consistent from ump to ump. I can tell in the first inning how well Jamie Moyer is going to do based on what the ump is giving him. There were games last year in the Milwaukee series in the playoffs where the ump was giving him nothing. I honestly think that the guys who have been around a little bit, who have proven they can hit the corners, should not be squeezed.

It used to be that if you had a pitcher throwing 80 mph, he wouldn't make the ump work hard because he would be around the plate, like Greg Maddux or Tommy John. Eventually, he might get a call 5 or 6 inches off the plate. Why? Because that pitcher has spent 20 years proving he could throw it there wherever he wants. You won't find a hitter in the game that has a problem with that, as long as what is a strike in the first inning is a strike in the ninth.

I think it is an injustice when a pitcher like Moyer gets forced into the middle of the plate. I think the more time you put into your job, the more you have earned. You have paid your dues. Don't call a game like he's a rookie still searching for the strike zone. Umps don't recognize this as much as they used to, and I think it is wrong.

Now I was wild. Every ump knew it, and every hitter knew it. I did not expect to get borderline calls, and I didn't. I knew what was going on. That was all my responsibility. I never blamed the umps for that.

It's the same with a free swinger. You can't swing at a pitch a foot outside then complain when you get rung up on a pitch an inch or two off the black. "Son," the ump is telling the hitter, "if you thought that pitch you just swung at that was a foot outside was good enough, then don't expect a break when you let one go by on the borderline."

The thing that cracks me up is when a guy swings at a pitch for strike three, then turns around and asks the ump, "Was that a strike?" What he just did was remove any credibility he had. It reveals that the hitter is still learning, and believe me, there are a lot of pitchers more than capable of teaching those hitters many lessons.

Pitchers and hitters alike just want to know what a strike is and keep it like that the whole game. But some umps are inconsistent, no doubt, and players *hate* that. Nobody cares about the size of an ump's strike zone if it stays the same.

I remember back in the NLCS versus the Braves. Joe West was behind the plate, and Mark Lemke was up. I went 3–1, and I had thrown one ball out of the strike zone by my calculation. I threw a fastball down the middle of the plate at the knees that he called a ball. Then I threw one down the middle, thigh high, that he called a ball. You begin to think, "If those are balls, where do I have to throw it to get a strike called?" I ended up getting him out, but geez, what's a guy got to do?

There are a lot of pitches on the border that I think should be called strikes and are not. That's why the games take so long. You can't force pitchers to throw only down the middle. That's not baseball; that's batting practice.

You want to know why there are so many home runs? One reason is steroids, sure, but a big reason is you can't pitch inside anymore. A hitter can eliminate half the plate.

No wonder pitchers will seek anything that will distract the batter. Until they made it illegal, pitchers wore gold chains around their necks, which would flutter and, during day games, reflect sunlight. Now pitchers have to wear their jewelry inside, except for those copper necklaces a lot of guys wear today, which don't seem to flutter or sparkle, so nobody cares about them. I guess they are a New Age remedy that keeps the blood healthy and all your energy flowing in the right direction. It couldn't hurt.

Fluttery sleeves, baggy uniforms, light T-shirts, anything that distracts the batter can be removed by the umpire. Yet the biggest distraction to a batter, aside from the break and speed of the pitch itself, can never be taken away—the pitcher's motion.

Sure, Tom House got me to the majors partly by cutting down my motion to its essentials so I could repeat it again and again. This has been the teaching trend since at least the 1950s, when Larsen and Turley's no-windup motions proved to be decades ahead of the herd. You got a guy who lacks command? Pare down his motion.

But sometimes a little more windup can help. It can help you get into a little better rhythm. You rock back so you can come forward, get a little momentum going. This can also provide a bit more distraction for the hitter. He can get focused on watching you windup and then have just a bit more trouble finding your release point. When fractions of seconds make the difference between hits and misses, a little more motion might be worth it.

During spring training, Justin Verlander struggled to get outs, but he didn't care. He was trying something new, using more of a windup. The Tigers right-hander had a disappointing 2008 season, at least partly because he lacked command and tended, once he got hit a little, to work too fast. Winding up more was intended to focus him, slow him down, and provide something else for the hitters to look at. It worked big time. After a few early struggles, he dominated more than ever.

Paring down your motion is also supposed to make you quicker to the plate to keep base runners from stealing. That's a worthy goal but only to the point that you don't sacrifice stuff to be quick. You can get pared down too much. That's why I hate the slide step. Sure you're quicker, but what does it matter if the runner on first doesn't get a good jump if the batter hits your pitch into the bleachers?

It's the same with fielding. I didn't end up in exactly the best spot to field my position, but it was how I ended up when I threw the ball as hard as I could. I'm a huge believer in putting as much on the baseball as possible. A pitcher's most important job is getting the hitter out. You get the hitters out and you don't have to worry that they will steal.

It's like what Dizzy Dean told writers when they asked him if he had a good pickoff move. "I don't know," he said. "Don't nobody get to first often enough for me to find out."

Nobody needs to resort to the slide step because anybody can come up with a good pickoff move with practice. Really, you don't even need that. You just have to be able to hold 'em close. You talk to any good base stealer, and he will tell you that the main thing is that he doesn't want his timing messed up.

You can hold the ball. You can look over to first. You can change your timing to the plate. Throw over. If you use a slide step, and use it with the same rhythm every time, you are just defeating the whole purpose.

With me, my leg kick was such that my knee would cross my post leg, but my foot never did. So that put me in a natural position to go to first, and it would be just short of a balk.

Eventually somebody will hit the ball to you, or to first, and you will have to become a fielder. That's where PFP, Pitchers' Fielding Practice, becomes important. Some pitchers hate it. I never did. Heck, I enjoyed everything that had to do with the game. I thought players who didn't enjoy fielding practice didn't like the game enough.

What people don't like about it is that it is endless repetition, mostly in spring training. The idea is to have a pitcher so trained that he naturally does it right without thinking. You run the proper route to first to take a throw from the first baseman. You field bunts and set up to throw so you don't toss a slider to first. You see a pitcher throw a bunt into the stands, he thought about it.

The toughest fielding play for a pitcher is the 1-6-3 double play. First, you have to remember who is running and how hard the ball is hit before you decide to throw to second or go for the sure out at first. Then you have to throw to nobody. That is, you throw to a spot above second base well before the infielder is there. It is hard to throw there with no target. You throw to nothing, trusting that he will be there.

You also have to remember where the infielders are positioned in order to gauge whether or not one of them can get to the bag in time. If Jim Thome, a slow runner, is up with a man on first and hits a grounder back to the pitcher, you might think that is an easy double play. But infielders use a huge shift when Thome is up. The third baseman is usually playing in the shortstop hole, and the other three infielders are way back on the grass and shifting for him to pull. A pitcher can get a grounder, but by the time someone gets to second for the force, Thome is likely to be impossible to double up.

That's the consequence of the extreme shifts used today. All fielders are placed much more precisely now because there is such an immense amount of data. Every hit by every batter is known by every team. Still, a pitcher holds, or ought to, the final decision on where his fielders ought to play. I always had a feeling for what a hitter would do off me. It was not necessarily what the data said he usually did. If I knew a certain hitter wasn't going to get around on me, and he was a righty, I told the right side of the infield to be heads up because I knew what I was going to throw to him.

The really distorted shifts are all against lefty pull hitters: Giambi, Delgado, Ortiz, and Thome. The second baseman is 20 feet out on the grass! Just about every game, one of these guys hits some laser through the infield, and the second baseman catches it on two hops without moving and throws him out by four steps. All of these guys would be hitting around .320 without those shifts.

Right-handed pull hitters don't get shifted against so extremely for the simple reason that if a shortstop played that deep, he couldn't throw out the runner anyway. They might be able to get away with putting three infielders on the left side of the infield more often than they do, as long as they didn't play too deep.

Shawon Dunston was the exception to this when we played with the Cubs. He used to play Jack Clark at least 10 feet into the outfield grass. Ken Caminiti played pretty deep because his rifle arm allowed it. Brandon Inge could probably play deeper than he does.

Tulowitzki and Furcal get away with playing deep, too.

Defenses don't just shift according to charts that say a certain hitter usually hits one way or another. The real live game must be taken into account, too. For instance, both Ryan Howard and Chase Utley hit a large number of ground balls to the right side of the infield. Howard gets shifted, and Utley doesn't. Why?

If you look at Chase, he stands on the dish. Every hitter protects his weakness, which means he has trouble with the ball away. So they try to pitch him away. Defenses are not going to play the infield for him to pull when they are pitching him away. They just will not do it.

It has to do with his power. He will hit that outside pitch for a single sometimes, but just about all his homers are pulled. The defense isn't aligned only according to where they hit the ball most but where a hitter will do the most damage.

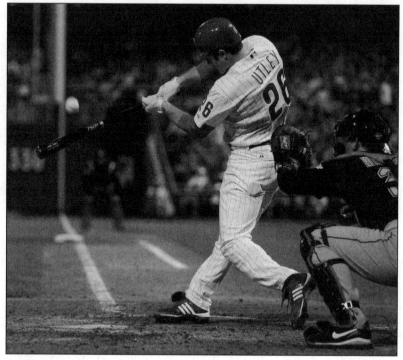

Chase Utley of the Phillies is shown here at bat against the Florida Marlins on October 2, 2009.

Ryan is just the opposite. He stands way away from the plate, but he is quick inside. He can hit the inside pitch out, like Utley, but he will also take the ball middle out and hit a homer to left. They try to keep the ball down on him. They do *not* want to pitch him outside, so they can shift the defense.

You have to be consistent. Toronto was playing Greg Dobbs to pull in a game around July 4, 2009, but the pitcher was throwing everything away. One, the pitcher has to be aware of his defense and pitch to it or change it. Second, Dobbs can also go the other way. He hit a little flare over short for a single. Little things like that can cost ballgames.

Nobody is more important defensively than the catcher, especially to a pitcher. If a pitcher doesn't have to stand out there and shake all night long, it lets him get into a rhythm. There are catchers who work well with pitchers. They know what the pitcher wants to throw, when and where he wants to throw it, and to whom. Other catchers don't do as much homework. Some catchers don't know the hitters as well, so they can't help as much. And some catchers are just not as creative about pitch selection. You can guess right along with some catchers. They never fool you. Others seem to always call for fastballs when the hitter is guessing curve, and vice versa. Those are the catchers you want in your games.

Working hitters is important, but there are only so many options available. Texas Rangers fan and Boston-area baseball radio voice Bill Barton discovered this when he interviewed Red Sox catcher Tony Peña in the early 1990s. Bill wanted to know how Peña would pitch to A's slugger Jose Canseco.

"Fastballs high and tight, breaking stuff low and away," Tony replied. And how would he pitch to his teammate, the other Bash Brother, Mark McGwire?

"Fastballs high and tight, breaking stuff low and away," Tony repeated.

Bill was beginning to detect a pattern. "How would you pitch to God?" Barton queried.

"Fastballs high and tight, breaking stuff low and away," the veteran catcher said. "And He knows it's coming."

Why wouldn't every catcher know the hitters well? It's homework. Why didn't all the kids you went to school with all do their homework? It's extra work. Plus, some guys have real good baseball intellects while others don't. Some catchers work very basically, and others know the game on a much higher level.

Darren Daulton was really good with me. He knew me as well as anybody ever has. He knew everything I wanted to do. There was not a whole lot of shaking going on when I was out there with him. See the sign, and let it go.

The mechanics of catching are important, too. I didn't have to worry too much about catchers blocking pitches in the dirt because I pitched up—up and in. But guys like Brad Lidge need somebody like Carlos Ruiz, who blocks the low pitch as well as anyone I've ever seen. Brad has to have the confidence to throw that big breaking slider in the dirt and know that it's going to be caught.

A catcher's arm is important but not as important as it is made out to be. All major-league catchers have a good enough arm to throw people out if you give them a chance—99 percent of all bases are stolen off the pitcher, and the catcher does not have a chance. It's up to the pitcher to throw over, keep the runner thinking, and make his throws to the plate in decent time. If the runner is kept uncomfortable, he's not going to get a good jump. He might not go at all. Using the percentage of runners caught stealing to judge catchers is very, very misleading.

In golf, they say you drive for show and putt for dough. In catching, you throw for show but block the plate and call the game for dough.

Another position where pitchers like to see a good glove is first base, which is a vastly underrated defensive position. From the Pony League on, teams want to put their big donkeys at first. Pitchers hate that, even when the donkey can hit.

When I think of first-base defense, I think of Mark Grace. He was a lot of fun to watch when I came over to the Cubs. He was the consummate ballplayer, what you call a pretty boy. Every team has one. He was a good-looking guy. They loved him in Chicago. He was a crowd favorite, and he could hit. He wasn't going to hit a lot of homers, but it was fun watching him. He could put the bat on the ball, but he was an even better fielder. Tremendous. I don't think he ever got enough attention for his fielding.

The kind of first baseman that Grace was is falling out of fashion because of the number crunchers. The most homers he ever hit in one year was 17. In seven of the years he was a regular, his homer total didn't even get into double digits. Almost no first baseman would keep his job doing that today. A Mark Grace is often undervalued by fans, especially fans that don't see him every day. But now it seems the Grace-type player is being undervalued by management, too.

If I have the opportunity to put a good glove in the field, I'm going to take it because I'm a pitcher. A first baseman like Grace over a season might make the difference in a hundred outs. You

Cubs first baseman Mark Grace tags out Darryl Hamilton of the San Francisco Giants on a pickoff play at first base in the fifth inning on May 11, 1997, in San Francisco. (AP Images)

had Shawon Dunston, throwing 100-mph lasers in the dirt at first and Grace coming up with them easily. Easily. That's invaluable. I look at a first baseman the same as I do a catcher. A good defensive performer is going to help us win more than a mediocre fielder with a bigger bat.

Bill Mazeroski got into the Hall of Fame a few years ago primarily because of the rise of some statistics that were able to show his value in the field. Some people concluded that he had been the greatest fielding second baseman in history, maybe the greatest defensive player, period. Now maybe he was and maybe he wasn't, but defensive statistics are still hard to quantify and make meaningful, and for first basemen and catchers, it is even worse. The percentage of base stealers a catcher throws out is more a factor of the pitcher's ability to hold 'em close than it is a catcher's arm. There is no stat for first basemen for "numbers of throws caught that otherwise would have gone into the dugout."

Keith Hernandez was the only guy I ever saw who could influence a game by the way he played first base. He would charge like a third baseman and throw a runner out at second or third, even on a good bunt. I would not be surprised if at some time in the future somebody develops some computer program that shows that Keith Hernandez's glove helped his team to win as much as Darryl Strawberry's bat. Then Keith will get in the Hall of Fame by some Old Timers vote.

After watching thousands of baseball games, you sometimes get a kind of intuition about what you need to do that wins baseball games that is not quantifiable, at least not yet. Those guys like Grace and Hernandez make it look so easy that nobody thinks it's spectacular. That's the problem. The average fan just says, "Oh. He caught the throw."

Gracie is also the guy who said that I "pitched like my hair was on fire." It stuck with me, and stuck in the language. The "like his hair is on fire" has become a well-worn cliché, and if Mark didn't use it first, he was close. So the next time you hear it, remember what it really means is that somebody does something the way I pitched—all out. Thanks, Mark.

No pitcher can just depend on his catcher doing homework, no matter how good that catcher is. No pitcher can depend on the defense to be positioned correctly without the pitcher knowing how his stuff works against a given hitter. At pitchers' meetings, you tell the other guys how you got a hitter out and listen to them. But one pitcher might say, "He can't get to the ball inside."

You might have to think to yourself, "Sure, he can't get to you inside. You throw 98 mph." It might not work for you. I watched hitters my whole career. That's all I did for the first six innings. I wanted to know where their holes were. Every hitter is a fastball hitter, but not every hitter can hit a fastball equally well in all four zones.

A starter needs to look at recent games of the team he's facing next to see who's hot and who's not. Then go back and look at how he did against that team, even going back to the previous year. Every hitter shows tendencies, but good hitters make adjustments, and young hitters who are going to be good start making them right away. A pitch you got a rookie out on last year might be a pitch he's killing now. You've got to know that. It doesn't seem to me that pitchers do this kind of homework as much as they used to. I think they depend too much on catchers and coaches to do it for them. Nobody can do it for you.

When I see some guys go out there and see them make the same mistakes again and again, I have to assume they are not watching much video. A perfect example is Raul Ibanez in the first half of 2009. I didn't think he was going to be all that great a pickup for the Phillies; then he goes out and does his Babe Ruth imitation, and I'm thinking, "Hey! This is a high-ball hitter; maybe they ought to try keeping the ball down." Yet he continually gets the ball up. I don't get it. He must think he died and went to heaven. If you get the ball middle to down, he might get a hit, but he's not going to hit it out of the park very often.

With interleague and divisional play, teams don't see each other as often as they used to. Maybe being the new kid on the block lasts a little longer now; a hitter comes over from the other league, and it takes longer for pitchers to adjust. But that is what video is for. You don't have to hit me in the face before I say, "Ya know what? This guy is a high-ball hitter."

Visits to the mound, whether by catchers, coaches or managers, are way less interesting than fans think. Usually they are just to remind a pitcher of the game plan he already went over. Sometimes it is just to break the timing of a hitter who looks like he's about ready to tee off on your heat or to slow down a pitcher who has is working too fast for his own good.

Darren Daulton never said anything about mechanics or the hitter. Dutch would come out and say, "Look. There is beer in the clubhouse. It is cold. Let's go. Get this over with." He wanted you to think about anything other than the predicament you were in. Same with our pitching coach then, Johnny Podres. Pod knew everything about every kind of pitch that was ever thrown. But visiting the mound is not the time for teaching. It was always just a little positive message that he brought to you to keep you focused, then he turned around and walked back.

Pulling a pitcher is usually not a surprise. You never admit it, but sometimes a pitcher is way more relieved to be relieved than he lets on. Sometimes not.

I was closing for the Cubs and Don Zimmer in 1989. They had just called up Les Lancaster from Triple A. He was a right-hander, and he started out like he was Superman. He threw about 33 consecutive scoreless innings of relief, setting up for me.

We were battling Montreal for the division lead. I was having good year and we got into the ninth inning leading 4–2. The heart of their batting order was coming up. I got Hubie Brooks on a fly, and then came Tim Raines and Tim Wallach. I knew what the manager was thinking. I better get Raines or Zimmer won't want me to face the righty Wallach as the tying run. Raines dumped a short line drive in front of Darrin Jackson, who was playing left.

Here comes Zim. I went into the dugout, and I just snapped. I threw my glove, cussed up a storm, and abused the water cooler, the usual. After the game, Zimmer called me into his office and said, "Don't you ever show me up like that again."

"Zim. I was not mad at you at all," I said. "I was mad at myself because I let Raines get a hit, knowing full well you were going to pull me if I did, because it was the right move." He thought I was upset at him. I had to explain to all the media guys, too.

Lancaster got the save. Zimmer made the right move. When you see guys going nuts in the dugout, it's usually because they are pissed at themselves.

Baseball fans seem to think that the guys out in the bullpen just eat, play pranks on each other, and generally cut up. Not really. I wouldn't even go down to the pen until after the sixth inning. I was usually inside the clubhouse watching the hitters on television or watching recent video of whatever team we were playing. I could get away with that because I only needed maybe three pitches to be ready. I had one of those arms. After I got ready, I stretched and tried to keep loose. I wouldn't throw any more. If they called for me really suddenly, I could just take the eight warm-ups on the mound and be ready. I'd say most pitchers needed 20–30 pitches in the pen, but it varied quite a lot from pitcher to pitcher.

Even if I wasn't going to pitch, once I got to the pen, I didn't do a lot of laughing and joking. I figured that even if I wasn't working that night, somebody else was, and he needed to focus, not crack up. You had to respect their need to prepare. I always thought you ought to watch the game.

No one liked to joke around more than I did, but I didn't think you should be cutting up when you should be watching the game so you were ready when you had to go in.

When I knew I might go in, I was always either stretching or going over the hitters. It's hard to come up with funny stuff when the game is on the line. There's a time and a place.

But you are a sitting duck for the fans, and they have a million ways to break your concentration. I've heard it all. They hated me in Boston because I was always knocking down Boggs and Greenwell. They had this little overhang in the Fenway Park bullpen. I had to stay under it or I'd get hit with all sorts of different stuff.

In Texas, I once hit three Orioles including two in a row. Earl Weaver charged the plate and screamed that I ought to be banned from the league. It came out in the papers the next day. He said I was more dangerous than smoking. The next time I warmed up in Baltimore, they threw hot dogs, pretzels, beer, anything they could. They had an old Volkswagen van to take guys from the pen to the mound, which I normally did not use. But that night you can be sure I rode in it. I had to take cover.

My first pitch hit Jim Traber right in the chest.

So I hit four Orioles in two games. It's a good thing none of those fans had a good enough arm to hit me with anything while I was on the mound. It was just one of those things. I wasn't *trying* to put guys on base. But I never blamed fans in any city. You have to let a lot slide off your back and understand that they are just rooting for their teams.

Yes, you do get fans in the stands that go out to the bullpen and want to talk and all. Yes, some of them are young women. And yes, they do converse about a wide variety of topics. I always just treated them as fans being fans and tried to focus on how I was going to pitch to Tony Gwynn. In San Diego, near the bullpen in Jack Murphy Stadium, they had a walkway that was placed next to the pen and several feet above it. Various females would walk by and sometimes just stand there. They would be in mini skirts, and we would be looking up and talking to them. "Oh, my gosh," we pitchers would say to ourselves. There are some pretty people in San Diego. Sometimes it is tougher to get the game face on than others.

Chapter Three

Life in the Majors

L ife in the big leagues wasn't a big adjustment for me at all. My first year in the majors was statistically better than any I ever had in the minors. I never had a minor league earned run average under 4.0, ever. My first year in the big leagues it was 3.58. That year the league average was 4.19.

When I got to the big leagues, I was already a reliever. I was able to do what I could do and didn't have to try and do it over six or seven innings. I could come in and just throw as hard as I could. I just never worried about anything. For me it was all about, "Give me the ball!" I want to pitch. I want to pitch every day. In my first few years, I was pissed if I didn't pitch that day. Most days I wasn't disappointed. I threw in more than half of the Rangers' games my first two years. I didn't care who the hitter was.

But some guys never make the transition. We had a couple of kids in Philadelphia when I first got there who never quite turned the corner. A youngster named Pat Combs was supposed to be all-world, but he got to the big leagues and never had any success. He pitched in the starting rotation one year, and didn't do too badly, but that was it: one year, plus a few others when he was up and down. But he killed in Triple A.

This game is all about adjustments. Whether it is your mechanics, your thought processes, your approach to hitters, whatever—if you can't make adjustments, you are not going to stay. For me, the key to sticking in the majors was belief. There isn't anybody else going to believe in you until you believe in yourself. I don't think Combs had belief in what he was doing. Whereas I might have sucked, I still believed in what I was doing! It's more of a mental or psychological thing. The only difference between the majors and the minors is adjustments and belief.

Al Kaline came up to the Tigers right out of high school in Baltimore. He was thrown into the starting lineup in 1954 and hit .276 with only four homers. The next year he won the batting title with .340 and 27 homers. He made adjustments, part of which was putting on 20 pounds of muscle. Years later, someone asked him why he never hit as high as .340 again. "I never saw those pitches again," he replied.

Once pitchers realized Kaline was no longer a skinny teenager but a legitimate home-run threat, they quit throwing him pitches just to see how far he could hit them. He adjusted to their adjustments and, though he never hit .340 again, he hit enough to make the Hall of Fame.

Adjustments on the field aren't the only ones a player has to make. There are all kinds of distractions in big-league life. I never cared too much about that stuff. Travel is just a necessary evil, though a heck of a lot less evil than 10-hour bus trips in the Texas League. Hotels were just places to sleep. I've watched guys who got all caught up in the big-league lifestyle. I did my share of enjoying it, too, but I never let it affect what I was able to do on the field. As soon as what happens on the field isn't the most important thing you are doing, you're going to have trouble.

Trust me. The hardest place to pitch in the world is Class A ball. You can knock a guy down five times and he'll just get back up because he's hungry to get to the big leagues. It's tough to scare a guy who's trying to get somewhere.

No matter where you are trying to get, there will always be a manager waiting. Obviously, a manager can make or break a career. What makes for a good manager is simple—good players. Casey Stengel managed for years without winning anything until he came to the Yankees. When he won his first World Series in 1949, he said, "I couldna done it without my players." That really says it all.

The most important thing a manager does is to understand the personalities of the people who work for him. Then he has to put them in situations where they can excel. It doesn't matter if it is baseball, business, anything. The successful baseball managers are the ones who know what makes their players tick.

Anyone can make the moves during the course of the game. That's not what is important, and it's not a skill that is hard to find. It's managing 25 personalities. The guy who can manage all 25 and keep them pointed in the same direction is the guy who is still managing in October.

There's always a way to reach somebody, even the guys with difficult personalities. And if there isn't, you don't want that player on your team. I learned when I managed in the minors that some guys you have to coddle; some guys you have to put your foot in their ass. There are guys you can yell at, and they will take it. Others will try to prove you wrong. And sometimes you find a guy who, if you yell at him, will curl up and quit. That's the manager's job or, at least, the most important part of it—figuring out with each of those guys what it will take to motivate and get the most out of them. It is not the same for every player.

Jim Fregosi was the best I ever played for because he gave everybody a specific role. He made the moves during a game that were necessary, but he didn't direct anybody to do anything during the game. We knew what to do. So he just let us go out and play our game. He gave us roles where he thought we would succeed and then left us alone. This enabled us to play loose and with confidence.

Fregosi was managing the White Sox when I came up with the Rangers. My first year I had eight saves, and most of them seemed to be against Chicago. I just wore them out. When the Phillies fired Nick Leyva 13 games after I got there, Roger McDowell and I were sharing closing duties. As soon as Jim took over, due to the success I had against the White Sox, he called me into his office and told me I was closing. I said fine.

The great thing about Jimmie is he'd give me the ball and all the rope in the world. I was either going to sink or swim, but he left it all on me. I think in '93 he might have come and got me about once all year. He built confidence in all his players like that. You hear players say about their manager, "He lets us play." This is what they mean. He gave us all jobs to do and then let us do them. He'd hand me the ball and go into the tunnel and smoke a cigarette.

He didn't have to police the team. We had Darren Daulton in the clubhouse. He did all the policing that was necessary. That sort of leadership from a player, somebody who has the respect of everyone on the team, helps a manager a lot. Fregosi never had to say a word to anybody. If you didn't bust your butt, somebody on that team would let you know in a hurry.

It comes down to knowing what your players are capable of doing. Charlie Manuel in Philadelphia is outstanding at this. He is one of those big ol' southerners with a drawl, and he is a lot smarter than some people think he is. He has a good sense of his own ego. Charlie does not care about *anything* but winning baseball games. He doesn't want any attention. He's never going to garner much, either. The only attention he gets is because of his accent and because he's an absolutely terrible television interviewee. He just doesn't like the camera. He gets nervous. He hates the spotlight. But you get him off by himself and let him talk baseball, and you very quickly find he's forgotten more about this game than most people will ever know. He's fine on radio, where he can't imagine a few million people looking at him. The worst thing you could do is assume he's ignorant because he has a southern accent and is not going to use big words. Believe me, he knows the game.

Bobby Valentine was just the opposite. He wanted all the attention on him. It didn't have anything to do with winning or losing. Sure, he wanted to win, but win or lose, it was all about, "Can I get the camera turned on me?" He never understood that a manager has something in common with an umpire—they should be seen and not heard. Or at least, the spotlight should get turned on them only when they screw up.

Do you think Joe Torre wants attention or needs it? He doesn't care about accolades or recognition or "where's the camera?" He wants to sit back, manage his ball club, and at the end of the year have people say, "Wow. He did a helluva job. He's a really good manager."

Now, as far as knowing the game of baseball, nobody is ahead of Bobby Valentine. The problem was that he was a terrible communicator with his players because he was always looking for attention. This may have been because his playing career was cut short by a gruesome leg injury before it even got started.

He was a phenomenal high school athlete. He was the first three-time All-State football player in Connecticut. He was a first draft choice of the Dodgers and reached the majors when he was only 19. He was part of a big trade to the Angels, when the Dodgers got Andy Messersmith. He was a .300-hitting center fielder when his spikes got caught in a chain-link fence in Anaheim Stadium while trying to flag down a Dick Green home run, causing a compound leg fracture. It is one of the most stomach-turning sports injuries ever captured on film. He was never the same player.

I think maybe because he never had the career he was supposed to have, never held the limelight the way he had as a high school star and a young phenom, he still tried to be the center of attention as a manager. I think that need for attention hurt him as a manager. If he had had a great career, maybe he would have gotten that out of his system. Or maybe not.

It's one thing for a manager to protect his players from the media, or deflect them with bullshit, like Tommy Lasorda did. It is another to be a manager who always wants to be on center stage. It doesn't work—at least not for long.

Bobby has had a lot of success as a manager in Japan. Some speculate it is because sarcasm doesn't translate well into Japanese.

As far as managing pitching goes, the most successful managers really count on their pitching coaches. Most managers weren't pitchers. Bud Black is one of the exceptions. All most managers know about pitching, as Jim Palmer said about Earl Weaver, is that they had a hard time hitting. The manager has to know the guts of each pitcher. The pitching coach has to know everything else.

Pitchers are liars when it comes to telling a manager when they are tired. Like most professional athletes, by both training and personality, pitchers want to play until they drop. You don't *want* a pitcher who wants to come out of a game. That's why the manager needs to have his mind made up before he even takes that first step out of the dugout. You can't trust the pitcher's opinion of his performance. He *always* thinks he can get one more guy out.

When managers go to the mound and don't take the pitcher out, it isn't because he's been talked out of it. He can help his pitcher a lot with a few well-chosen words. The only thing you want to make sure of as a manager is that nothing negative comes out of your mouth. When a pitcher is in trouble, the first thing he thinks is, "I can't do this," or "I can't leave a pitch out over the plate."

You don't want him thinking that way. He needs to think, "I need to put that pitch right *here*." So the manager goes out and says, "I need you to put that fastball outside right on the black. And I know you are going to do it."

Some Detroit fans think Jim Leyland has a magical way of visiting the mound, staying about 10 seconds, and then having the next pitch end up in a double play or strikeout for his Tigers. After the game, if the pitcher is asked what Leyland said, many times it is not even about the next pitch, exactly, but more along the lines of, "Don't worry about the bunt because this guy *can't* bunt." He relieves a bit of the pitcher's anxiety by showing him that the manager is thinking with and for him. All the pitcher has to do is focus on making his pitch. Which, of course, is the secret of good pitching. It is easy to lose focus during a game. A good manager helps a player refocus.

You want to go out there and give the pitcher something positive to think about. It doesn't always work out that way. Bill "The Spaceman" Lee tells a story about my old Cubs manager, Don Zimmer, when they were both with Boston. Lee was in a jam, and Zimmer came to the mound. "Don't let this guy hit a home run," he said.

As Lee tells it, this planted not something positive in his mind, but a doubt. "Home run?" Lee says. "Home run! Why does Zimmer think this guy might hit a home run? What should I do? I can't let him hit a homer!"

Next pitch. Over the wall. A manager may have all the doubts in the world, but you don't want him to share them with his players.

A lot of times a team will take on the personality of the manager. I truly believe this. Take Billy Martin, one of the smartest, most aggressive, and intense managers of all time. He took over from Bill Virdon, a laid-back guy who was later pretty successful in Houston but less so in the intensity of New York City.

When Martin came to a team, they always played smart, aggressive baseball and won. But the intensity soon burned itself out; his teams were mentally and physically exhausted, and he had to move on. That's why George Steinbrenner wisely replaced Martin down the stretch in 1978 with Bob Lemon, who was as relaxed as Martin was hyper. The team stayed tough but was able to exhale a little, and they went on to win it all.

Likewise, the Phillies that won the Series in 2008 absolutely took on the personality of its laid-back manager. I watched it all year. You could look in the dugout and never tell by looking at Charlie whether the team was winning or losing. Nobody *cared* more about winning than Charlie; he just didn't show it. It kept the team loose because the manager was in control.

Sparky Anderson would say, "These kids (meaning the players) all want to win the game before they play it. I tell them, 'Let's just play the game and we'll see who wins.'" That attitude keeps the players focused on the game and not obsessed with the result. Sometimes a team can want to win so badly, it keeps them from winning. They forget to just *play*.

The least important thing a manager does is all the strategy during a game—play the infield back, play the infield in, make out the lineup, double switch, pinch-hit, pitching changes, hit and run, starting rotation, etc. Basically, if broadcasters during a game are making a big deal over it, you can be sure it doesn't mean too darn much. Not to actually winning or losing. Not over 162 games.

There isn't much difference between the best manager and the worst when it comes to these sorts of things. Some stats expert figured out that the difference between the most efficient way to arrange your batting order and the worst, given that you don't do anything insane like lead off with your pitcher or hit Chase Utley eighth, *might* be one win.

Fans are right. They *could* do these things as well as the real managers. Everyone can see the obvious.

Of course, you want your leadoff hitter to have a high on-base percentage. I don't really care how he does it. Jimmy Rollins is not your prototypical leadoff hitter. But when that guy scores a run, the Phillies win a ridiculously high percentage of the time. The key is finding out where a player excels and putting him in a position to do it.

Some people make a big deal over how many strikeouts Ryan Howard has. Who cares! I don't care how he makes an out. A strikeout is better than grounding into a double play. His job, and he knows it, isn't to get on base and put the ball in play. His job is to drive in runs.

I'm not a big fan of jockeying lineups, using a hundred batting orders during a season. You want guys who come to the ballpark and know their roles, what is expected of them. You don't want them to have to think, "Who am I hitting behind today? Who is following me?" Because a player will think about every little thing that's different from game to game, and every new thought he has is just a little bit of energy taken away from his essential job of winning the game. I want to come to work and not have to worry about changing my game at all.

The only way a platoon situation works is if it's consistent and the manager sticks to it. Players want to know when they go home at night whether or not they are playing tomorrow. A guy on any job, and baseball is no different here, has to have the opportunity to prepare for his job. This is true for every player, starter or reliever, regular or sub. As long as you know what your job is, you can go out there and do it. Players don't like surprises.

I think bringing in a lefty to pitch to a lefty hitter and so on is way overdone. It's another example of "going by the book." If you go by the book, you won't get second-guessed, but it won't necessarily win you ball games, either. Teams have so many pitchers today whose "job" it is to get one batter out and take the rest of the day off, there's no roster space for the good pinch-hitter or defensive replacement that teams used to carry. So more guys have to play when they're banged up or play in situations where they should be sitting. The result is a game that isn't as well played.

Managers would pinch-hit for lefties against me, but I didn't care. I had a bit more success against lefties, but it wasn't a big difference. I actually hated throwing to left-handed batters. I hit most of them.

Don Zimmer is one of my all-time favorite people in the game, and he was one of my favorite managers. I absolutely loved Zim. I don't think he's ever drawn a paycheck outside baseball. He's what you call a lifer—he will finish his life out on the field somewhere. As a manager, he would try anything. One winter on the Cubs Caravan, I said to a group of fans, "They say I pitch like my hair is on fire. Well, Zimmer manages like his hair is on fire." Maybe after managing so long, that's why he didn't have much hair left!

Whatever notion came into his mind, he did it. If the team executed, he looked like a genius. When they didn't, everybody second-guessed him, naturally.

Zimmer loved to hit and run, bunt and squeeze. He was all about playing the game of baseball old school. He was just a guy who, when you showed up at the park, you knew what to expect.

He got his nickname "The Gerbil," which he hated, from pitcher Bill Lee when he was the manager of the Red Sox. He wasn't all that fond of the guy they called "The Spaceman," because Lee was the very opposite of traditional. But Lee insists he was being complimentary. Lee once called Billy Martin a rat or a weasel or something, and some reporter heard him and asked him then, what Zimmer was.

Lee supposedly said that Zim was lovable, like a gerbil, and the rest is history. I have to admit, with the chaw of tobacco Zimmer used to sport, one might possibly see the resemblance.

When he was a kid, he was supposed to be the successor to Pee Wee Reese at shortstop for the Brooklyn Dodgers. Then he suffered a couple of life-threatening beanings in the minors. He played in the big leagues for 12 years, never reaching his potential. He had a lot of power for a little guy and would have been years ahead of his time as a power-hitting shortstop.

In 1958, Ernie Banks hit 47 homers while playing shortstop for the Cubs, winning the MVP award. Zimmer and the Giants' Daryl Spencer were next among shortstops with 17 each.

A few years before, he played short down in Puerto Rico on maybe the best Winter League team of all time. He had a couple of guys named Mays and Clemente in the outfield. It was the same Santurce team I was on about 30 years later.

When I came over from Texas to the Cubs, I brought a football with me. Tom House had all of his Rangers pitchers throw a football during batting practice. He believed it loosened up our arms without stressing them. I believed in it. I loved it. It's a great exercise. But Zim is a traditionalist. To him, a football on a baseball field was like Bob Dylan going electric at the Newport Folk Festival. The first time he saw that football, I thought he was going to break out in hives. Right away he said, "There ain't gonna be any footballs on this field."

I said, "Fine. It's your team. Your rules." I had no problem with that, and I put it in my locker and sort of forgot about it. Then one day, I was at the park early, as always. I was down in the clubhouse alone, except for the clubhouse boy, and Zimmer was up the stairs in his office. I remembered the football in my locker. So the clubbie and I threw it back and forth in the clubhouse a few times.

As we were throwing it, I yelled, "Get that god-damned football out of the clubhouse!"

Just then Zim stuck his head out of his office and yelled, "Get your ass up here!" And he proceeded to lay into me. He screamed and hollered at me for about 10 minutes. After a while, I couldn't even understand what he was saying. It was like the adults talking in those *Peanuts* television cartoons, just noise.

Finally he stopped to take a breath and I said, "Are you done?" He said, "Yeah, I'm done."

"I'm the only one in the clubhouse," I told him. "I wouldn't show you up to any of the guys. I was just messing with you. If you want to holler at me because you're in a bad mood, go ahead, but this is stupid."

He leaned across his desk and yelled, "Well, I just had a damned root canal!"

I knew something was bothering him, because he wasn't like that.

Besides playing for Zimmer, I also really appreciated getting to know Andre "Hawk" Dawson, who might have been the classiest guy I ever played with. If I were going to take a kid to a baseball game and point to a guy and say, "This is how you are supposed to conduct yourself." I'd point to Hawk.

Dawson still has a shot at the Hall of Fame, but he should have made it easily years ago. He hit 438 homers and had 1,591 runs batted in. Both put him well within the top 40 of all time. Everybody says that hitting 500 home runs is almost a free pass to the Hall of Fame. Hitting only a few less than 500 should not be a barrier, especially when you brought so much else to the field in addition to power hitting.

It could also be that playing in Wrigley Field might have hurt his chances. It's likely the voters discount his big home-run totals as a Cub so much that it's almost working against him. Jim Rice

Andre Dawson hit one of his 438 career homers on April 16, 1991, against the Phillies. (AP Images)

getting in ought to help Dawson. Rice got help from the wall in Fenway for longer than Wrigley helped Dawson. And Andre was a good outfielder, too; he was a center fielder for a long time who could throw and steal bases.

It hurts him that the years when he was truly a five-tool player were played up in Montreal, where he was seen by four fans and a moose.

I felt the same way about Dale Murphy, one of the nicest people you will ever meet in your life. You meet some guys who are phony nice, but Dale was genuine. It was a thrill to play with him because I grew up right outside of Portland, and Dale went to Wilson High School in Portland and was a local legend.

Like Craig Biggio, he started out catching, then moved to center field. I don't know if working behind the plate hurt his knees or what, but they were the reason he could not sustain the kind of numbers that won him back-to-back MVP awards in 1982 and 1983.

In those years, most people considered Murphy a lock for the Hall of Fame. He had hit 310 homers by the age of 31 in 10 full seasons. His career only lasted five more painful years, when he added only 88 more homers to his total. His career was outstanding but not what it might have been.

When I first saw them in the Phillies' clubhouse, I was shocked. His knees were brutally beaten up. They were hard to look at. He could still hit, but he couldn't move at all like he used to. Terrible. His knees were almost as bad as Dawson's, who had the ugliest knees I ever saw in my life. Dale's were a close second.

I'd look at Hawk in the Cubs clubhouse and say, "Dude, you got a 25-year-old body from the waist up and 75-year-old legs!" And his feet, from fouling balls off for a few thousand games, were just as bad.

You play this game long enough, you are going to get beat up. Murphy and Dawson played when there was a lot of artificial turf, too. That just destroyed players. Going back to grass has definitely saved and prolonged careers. It's not even close. Turf was horrible on your back and terrible on all your extremities. You could literally play on a parking lot and there wouldn't be a bit of difference.

Every once in a while, you hear about a high school wanting to install artificial turf, even today. The reason given is that, because there are so many teams now—soccer and field hockey and rugby, in addition to football, and both boys and girls teams, that turf will keep the field playable without a lot of maintenance. Right. Put turf in your high school and what you save on groundskeepers you can pay to doctors, as they try to salvage your children's knees, backs, and arms.

Among the new generation of managers, Joe Girardi is a very intelligent guy, as most fans know. I'm not the least bit surprised that he is managing the Yankees. The "student of the game" cliché applies. A graduate of Northwestern, Girardi is intellectual, but he could play. He had a great arm. He was a rookie in 1989 when I arrived with the Cubs. He had a long career because he was a good defensive catcher and knew how to make the best use of the tools he had. You knew he was one of those guys who would be around the game long after he retired as a player.

He never hit a ton, .267 lifetime average with no power, but his glove was good and he was great with a pitching staff. He would move a runner, he was a good bunter, and he proved that you don't have to be a burner to be a good base runner. Even when he played, his brain was his best attribute. If there was ever a player who you could *see* thinking on a diamond, it was Joe.

Before November 2009, Yankees fans spent a lot of time wondering why they hadn't won it all since 2000. They often say they miss the grind-it-out approach of Paul O'Neil and Scott Brosius. I'm sure that's true, but the Joe and Jorge Posada catching duo helped a lot for two of those four years. Hey, when you have a genius defensive catcher teaching a great-hitting young catcher—that combination doesn't come along every year.

As a manager Giradi has a reputation for being a little rigid or militaristic. He seems to have relaxed a bit in his second year in New York. That might be his intention, but it might also be due to having guys like C.C. Sabathia on the team. Sabathia is one of

Joe Girardi's longevity as a player and his success as a manager come as no surprise to those who know how much thought he puts into the game. (AP Images)

those guys who competes 100 percent but also knows where and when to have fun. A couple of guys like that can make a big difference in how much a manager can allow himself to relax. Joe just wants things done the right way. The New York media got down on him toward the end of 2008 because they thought he had been less than forthcoming about some player injuries. He got a little hamstrung there because how much he is allowed to discuss that stuff comes directly from the front office.

The same thing happened early in 2009 when Alex Rodriguez came back after his hip surgery. Whenever Alex got a day off, it was a big media item as to who was in charge: Joe, the Yankees' front office, or A-Rod's doctors.

As much as anything, this was lack of finesse on Joe's part, because his tendency is to speak his mind. Joe Torre might not have been any more open about injuries, but the writers let Torre pass, because Torre had won. And won some more.

Now that Girardi has gotten his bones in New York, he will be fine. Dealing with the media in New York is not something you just wake up one morning and know how to do. You have to learn it and earn it. There's only one way to earn it with the Yankees—get that ring.

* * *

Once any player gets to the big leagues and his manager gets enough confidence to keep him around, there will still be constant challenges, and not all of them have to do directly with baseball performance. I'm talking beanballs, brushbacks, and brawls.

The Red Sox Wade Boggs and Mike Greenwell were guys that I knocked down a lot, but I never hit either of them. I was 21 when I came into the league, and when I missed to left-handers, it was up and in. Then in spring training my third year, a batboy came over to me during a game with Boston and handed me a note, and all it said was, "We are going to kick your ass." I guess they figured that I missed up and in a little too much, that I must be throwing at their lefties. I asked the batboy who sent it, and he just said a bunch of guys were into it.

I wrote back, "Oooooooh," as if I were really scared. Not.

The first game we faced Boston in Arlington, I come into the game to start the ninth inning behind 3–0. Oil Can Boyd and Wes Gardner had us shut out. Marty Barrett starts the inning with a single. Boggs is up next, and he already had three hits. I'm trying not to make it four and balk. Barrett goes down to second and the third-base umpire, Ken Kaiser, comes all the way to the mound and says, "You got a problem with this team?"

"What are you talking about?" I ask.

"Well," Kaiser says. "I've never seen this before." I ask him what is he talking about, and he points to the Red Sox dugout. John McNamara had called his whole bullpen down, and the whole team except for Marty and Wade were standing on the top step of the dugout. It was like he called for reinforcements or something. I looked at Kaiser and said, "You know. I might have a problem with this team at that."

So my first pitch knocks Boggs down and Barrett starts running his mouth at second base. I tell him, "Look, if I ever knock you down, please, *please* charge the mound."

Rice flies to right and Marty takes third. Then Dewey Evans hits another fly, and Barrett heads home and I'm backing up the plate. He scores. I time my walk back to the mound to cross in front of him at home plate. I say, "Come get me," and just keep walking. As I'm walking, I look up at the Diamond Vision and see him coming to get me. So naturally, I turn around and start walking toward him.

John Shulock is the home plate ump. He comes out and grabs me. Barrett's still chirping and our third baseman, Steve Buechele, gets him around the waist. I keep inching my way toward Barrett and break free of Shulock. I get to Marty right at their on deck circle. I took my shot and hit him one right across the face. I knew I was only going to get one shot, since I was so close to their dugout.

Dewey grabbed me. That is a guy you do not want pinning your arms back. But I wrestled for four years, so I didn't let Evans get me on the ground where everybody could pound me. Just as I get loose from Dwight, Jim Rice tackles me, and *does* bring me down. Al Bumbry, their third-base coach, has both my arms behind my back, and Rice is flogging me. That is my most vivid memory of Jim Rice.

I got Charlie Hough trying to pull Rice off of me. Hough is like 108 years old and built like Walter Brennan.

I never once in my career hit Boggs or Greenwell. Their whole team got their panties twisted because I *came close*. This kind of stuff is what causes umpires to issue warnings when you just come close to a guy. That's a joke. In the generation before mine, you had guys like Don Baylor who understood the game. You could hit Baylor wherever you wanted to hit him as long as you didn't get up around his head. He understood you had to pitch him inside and that he was going to get hit on occasion. He was fine with that. Getting hit was part of his game. It was like, "I'm going to stand my ground. Go ahead and hit me. It won't bother me a bit. Won't drive me off the plate one inch."

Hell, you can *stand* on the plate it you want. I understand. He wants to cover the outside part of the plate. But if you stand on the plate, you are going to get hit. I would never throw at anyone's head, but I am going to try and get the ball in on guys.

You take the inside away from pitchers and it hurts the game so badly. There were a lot of reasons the offensive numbers blew up in the 1990s and later, but this was a huge reason. You see guys taking the ball 6 inches outside and hitting them out. You never saw that before. That didn't happen. If the hitter doesn't have some sort of fear of the baseball, he's gong to hit it hard. Umpires have taken that completely away from pitchers. They use no common sense. I've seen warnings on the first hitter of a game. You make that hitter move his feet, think about the inside pitch, and I don't care if he's as pumped as Arnold Schwarzenegger, he's not going to take a pitch 6 inches outside and hit it out the other way.

I made it known to all: you can charge the mound. You may win. I may win, but I will then hit you every time you come to bat. You want to fight? Remember I am the one holding the ball. I hit 52 batters in my career. I was never charged once. They knew I was wild, but I wasn't trying to hit people. It wasn't anything personal.

Calvin Schiraldi was on that Red Sox team that mortally hated me, and he was predisposed to continue hating me when we became teammates on the Cubs a few years later. He thought I always acted like I did on the mound! When we became teammates, we became the best of friends. Still are. Funny how things work out.

He gave me the nickname "Wild Thing" We saw *Major League* together when it first came out. Yes, I got my nickname from the pitcher that Charlie Sheen played; he didn't get the nickname from me. Except I didn't need glasses, which he needed in order to throw strikes in the movie. I need glasses now, though, and the only thing wild about me is that nickname. Really.

I guess having all the Red Sox come charging out of the dugout at once at least proved they had "good chemistry." Or maybe it proved that they needed 25 Red Sox to take on one Texas Ranger. Whatever. In any case, "chemistry" is one of those words that you hear all the time on radio sport shows and trust me; you never hear it in the dugout.

Chemistry is very simple. To me, it's just 25 guys on the same end of the rope. Simple to say but difficult to find.

You might not think about it, but there is a lot of diversity in the dugout. On every big-league club, you will find players of different races from different countries speaking different languages. Whatever chemistry is or is not, it for sure does not depend on the racial, ethnic, or educational mix of the players. Not at all.

Even within racial or ethnic groups, you have diversity. Some guys might be city guys, others country. Some are highly educated, and others didn't finish much school in any language. Some guys you'd trust to take care of your children. Others you wouldn't want to walk your dog.

In all my days in baseball, I don't think I saw a single flare-up because of racial or educational differences. One reason is that baseball has been integrated longer than many segments of society. Also, baseball is not about your race or education. It's not about where you came from. It's about "can you play?"

There is a lot more Spanish spoken in the clubhouse than there used to be, and more Japanese every year. I have seen how language barriers affect some players. But on every team now, there are players who are bilingual with Spanish and English. As long as there is somebody to help you understand things, you can function.

It helps to have a bilingual coach, sure, and a lot of teams do. It would help a manager, too, but it is not a necessity. As long as a manager has somebody to translate, he will be fine. Teams are also now taking steps to teach English to the young Latin guys they sign. A lot more players are bilingual these days.

I used to feel bad for the guys who couldn't speak English. They were lonely. They were a long way from home. I played with one kid in San Diego who was 15! Imagine sending your son to a foreign country not speaking the language. Of course, some of those 15-year-olds were really 19, but that's another story.

Back in the 1950s, writers would interview somebody like Roberto Clemente, who was brilliant, and they would write what he said like, "I heet ze ball." It made them sound funny. That wasn't right. Even today, I think some Latin players have to fight against the Latin stereotype. They get criticized for being lazy or being hot dogs when it's just a cultural difference. It doesn't affect how hard they play one bit.

Most players have experience playing with a lot of different folks even before they turn pro. It wasn't true for me, however. There were only two Black kids and no Latinos in my high school in Oregon. I went from that school right to my first professional clubhouse with all kinds of people, but it never bothered me. I was raised not to judge people that way. I just wanted to have fun and play. I could never understand how a person could look at someone else or listen to him and pass judgment on that basis alone. You really do not see much of that around baseball anymore. I never cared about anything except how somebody treated me and my teammates. When I managed, all I cared about was effort on the field.

So unlike a lot of areas of society, baseball doesn't suffer much at all from the kinds of racism or prejudice you can still find in a lot of other places. When John Rocker said those lunk-headed things a few years ago, part of the reason it was news is that you just don't hear baseball players saying that crap any more.

So chemistry isn't about getting along racially or speaking the same language or how much money you have or how you spend it. No matter who is on your team, if you got 10 guys going one way and 10 going another and five standing around, your team is going nowhere. I don't care how much talent you have. That's bad chemistry.

Chemistry is a trust. I've only been on two teams in my entire career that had great team chemistry: the '89 Cubs and the '93

Phillies. Some people say winning makes good chemistry. I think that's backward, although teams with good chemistry still might not have enough talent to win a pennant. Sometimes a team with great chemistry might be doing great to finish .500 because they don't have the horses. But chemistry *and* talent: that's what it takes. A lot of talented teams never win anything.

For instance, in 1992 the Phillies finished last. The next year we won the pennant; we won 27 more games. Yet that team didn't go out and sign free-agent super-stars to mega contracts. We didn't suddenly have a couple of rookies become All-Stars. We just got a few more good baseball players, and that lifted all of us to a higher level.

Lee Thomas was the general manager then. He was a hard-nosed bulldog. I mean, we went at it a couple of times. What I respected about Lee is that he still had that player's mentality. He came up through the Yankees' system and was touted as a future star. He made the team in 1961 and would have been witness to the Mantle-Maris home-run derby had he not been traded to the expansion Los Angeles Angels after two games. The next year he drove in more than 100 runs, becoming one of the Angels' first All-Stars.

Lee called a few of us into his office after the Phillies finished stinking in 1992: Kruk, Dykstra, Daulton, and me. It was, shall we say, an open discussion. We were screaming at each other. I told him there was no way we could win because we didn't have the players to win. Then he lost his temper, and I lost mine. But to even have a general manager invite his players to have their say is very, very unusual.

Later, Fregosi asked me if I had the chance to get Pete Incaviglia, would I do it? Pete never surpassed the 30 homers he hit his rookie year with Texas. He fell out of favor there and had kicked around from Detroit to Houston as a part-timer the last few years. I said, "I'd get him in a heartbeat. I watched the guy go from being one of the worst outfielders in creation to a pretty good one two years later. He will hit 30 homers by mistake if you keep him in the lineup. He will run through a wall for you. He plays as hard as anyone you will ever manage. I'd love to see Inky here." Thomas signed him as a free agent. He drove in 89 runs platooning with Milt Thompson.

Danny Jackson was taken by the Marlins in their original expansion draft. He had won 23 games and finished second in the Cy Young voting in 1988 with the Reds. Since then, he had fought arm problems, so we were able to get him for two prospects. He went 12–11 for us, which doesn't seem like much, until you realize the guy he replaced went 1–14 the year before.

We got Jim Eisenreich. David West. Larry Andersen. Just plain good baseball guys. Kevin Stocker developed as a rookie shortstop and hit .324. Lee got a bunch of guys that fit his mold. Winning, and the chemistry that goes along with it, isn't always about superstars. It is about guys who go out every day and leave it all on the field.

Eisenreich was a really interesting story. He was a tremendous talent who struggled with Tourette's Syndrome. Back when it was troubling him, I think it was the first time a lot of people had even heard of it. Sometimes it even kept him from playing because he was 30 years old before he got into as many as a hundred games in any one season, and it surely was not because of lack of playing ability.

Even when he had it under control, it was hard for him to fit in because people tended to treat him with kid gloves, not knowing how to talk to him. The Phillies did not have any kid gloves. Five minutes after he walked into our clubhouse, Kruk was doing an interview and a writer asked him about Eisenreich's joining the team, given he had Tourette's Syndrome. Kruk summed it up perfectly: "Tourette's Syndrome! We got a bunch of guys in this clubhouse way more fucked up than he is!"

So from the first day, Eisy learned that we were not going to treat him like a special-needs outfielder. If somebody had a malady on our team, it was pointed out to him on a daily basis. You didn't treat anybody differently.

Right before Kruk discovered he had testicular cancer, back at the end of 1993, we were playing a game in Los Angeles. When it gets late out there, a heavy dew sits on the grass. Somebody bunted on me, I fielded it and threw a missile to first. The throw skipped off the wet grass and hit John right in the cup, which blew up. Just shattered like porcelain. That winter he was still hurting, so he went to the doctor, thinking it was my throw causing it, and that's how the testicular cancer was discovered. So they went in and removed the testicle. Good thing I bounced that throw.

The next spring, after he goes through radiation treatments, he wants to play opening day. He's pleading his case, but they don't want to play him. They thought he might not be ready. The next day, Larry Anderson puts a T-shirt in his locker that says, "If I'm not playing, I'm taking my ball and going home."

Nothing was off limits. Whatever bad happened to anybody, humor was the cure on that team.

Eisenreich said that it was the first time he ever felt like just a regular guy. How could we *not* accept him? The man played four years in Philadelphia and hit .324. He was a really good guy, who could flat out rake. Had it not been for the Tourette's, there is no telling how good he could have been. He wasn't a big power guy; he was a pure hitter. He could run; he could do everything well. A winning team needs these kinds of players. Another guy might lead the league in something and get more publicity, but unless they have some all-around players like Jim, a team won't win much.

Larry Andersen was a joke looking for a place to happen. We used to make fun of him because Boston traded him for Jeff Bagwell. Boston got a total of 22 excellent innings from Larry at the end of 1990, which helped them into postseason play and won them the privilege of being swept by Oakland.

Houston got 449 homers from Bagwell.

All Larry threw were sliders, but he did his job. He was a practical joker who had fun playing the game until the day he quit. The MLB television network did a program that included him as one of the top baseball characters of all time. It showed me helping him with his thinning hair by spraying on that stuff that is supposed to darken the thin spots and make hair look fuller. He ended up looking like his head got stuck in a bucket of paint.

Larry loved life and still does. But don't ask me about his practical jokes. They are too gross to want to remember, let alone write down.

Good chemistry is just one of those things you either have or you don't. It's not something you can go out and create. That's why when you find it, you better make the most of it. There has to be a complete unselfishness in the way everybody goes about their business.

A manager or a general manager can have a big impact on chemistry by adding or subtracting players. Branch Rickey had a strategy called "addition by subtraction." He meant that sometimes a team plays better just by getting *rid* of a particular player. It all comes down to the character of the individual player. If I'm the manager or the GM, I want players who want to win.

But doesn't everybody want to win? Trust me, there are a lot of guys whose first and foremost thought is not about the outcome of the game. I played with Curt Schilling. If his team went 20–142, but he had the 20 wins, that would be all he cared about.

Schilling is not my favorite guy in the world, as is well documented. If I had a big game to win, I'd want him to pitch it. But he would not be at my table on Thanksgiving Day. In 1993, Curt won 16 games and I saved 12 of them. You know how many of his potential wins I blew? Zero. So when we are in the World Series and he puts a towel over his head when I come into pitch, well, that kind of stuff is just unforgivable as far as I'm concerned. I told him point blank: "You're a great pitcher. But sooner or later, you can't pitch anymore and you'll have to be a man, and you ain't a very good one."

There have been television shows about Curt where he says that I was the only teammate he ever had that didn't like him, and that is just a bold-faced lie. I'm just somebody that will speak his mind. I will speak the truth whenever there is a chance. I don't go out of my way to bury a guy. I always say that Schilling was one helluva pitcher. When he took the mound, you knew you had a good chance to win. But as for the rest of it you've got to be there for the team, not just yourself.

Yet in 1993 the Phillies had great chemistry, even with a guy like that. How was that possible? Everybody understood him and kept him in check while he was there. Guys wouldn't let other guys get bugged by his behavior.

The same thing happened with the Red Sox. There were a lot of strong personalities on that team. You can overlook or ignore Schilling's personality when a team is going good. If you have a couple of guys who are hard to get along with, and everybody knows it, the rest can all work around it together. The thing that neutralizes it is *winning*! But you put a guy like Curt on a team that is struggling, or doesn't have some strong positive personalities, and I guarantee it, there will be blood.

Sometimes you see a team get a guy, or get rid of someone, and you know it had more to do with chemistry than performance.

Milton Bradley is an unbelievable baseball player. He's played with seven teams in 10 years because he's a pain in the ass. He played all of 2008 with Texas and had his best year. He moved to the Cubs for 2009. He will be elsewhere in 2010. There are guys who play great, and after awhile you just decide, "We're going to have to make do without him and his antics."

The Dodgers probably would not have gone to the postseason without Manny Ramirez in 2008, but the Red Sox probably would not have gone *with* him. Now with his steroid suspension, and the Dodgers having such a great record without him, it is hard to tell what affect the guy is really having or going to have. That's why chemistry is a great topic of conversation among fans but not players.

There is no player who is so talented that you have to put up with the intolerable, although if you look around, you can see that not everyone agrees with me. I still think that, although you might miss what a bad actor contributes, the whole team will be relieved, play looser and better, and win more.

If there were a kind of player that improves chemistry, it would be someone like John Kruk. I've known Kruky longer than I've known anyone else in baseball. I signed with the Padres a year after he did, so he was always a classification ahead of me. We went to San Diego spring trainings together in Yuma, Arizona, then I'd go to A ball, and he would get sent to Double A, and so on. I got taken in the Rule 5 draft after 1984 and switched to Texas. He stayed with the Padres and got to the show in 1986. I got there the same year with the Rangers. So I didn't run into him for a few years until he got traded to the Phillies and I was on the Cubs.

Kruk was always heavy, but nowhere near as heavy as he was at the end of the career. One thing most people don't realize about John, is that he could really run. Think about it: if he could only run as fast as he looked like he could run, he could never have played big-league ball! You watch him long enough, and you begin to see what an exceptional athlete the guy is, regardless of what he looks like. He was a tremendous basketball player and golfer. He could fall out of bed Christmas morning and double off the wall. He finished his 10-year big-league career with a batting average of exactly .300. He was just a country boy from West Virginia, a very down-home guy, and he was one of my all-time favorite people in the game.

The story about John that says a lot about him has become pretty famous. He was smoking a cigarette, walking out of a hotel one night, and a woman came up to him and said, "You shouldn't be smoking cigarettes, you're an athlete."

Kruk said, "I ain't no athlete, lady, I'm a ballplayer."

John always had a great sense of humor. That's one reason why he's so popular on television today, of course. But he also always wanted to play the game the right way. We came up toward the end of the 1980s, when there were still some guys around from the '70s, and we learned to play the right way from them. When you were a rookie, you just shut up and went out and played.

Now the game has changed so much. It you look down the dugout before a game, there will be guys on their cell phones and all. If you want to talk on your cell phone in the clubhouse, that's one thing. Once you walk on the field, I don't want to see any electronics. I just have no time for that. I hate that.

I don't understand how guys can do that. For me, the field was a place I could escape. Somebody once said the great thing about riding a motorcycle is that is *all* you are doing. It takes all your attention. No room for distraction, unless you want to end up in the ditch. I feel the same way about baseball. Once you go on the field, it should be all about the game. Even during batting practice and warm-up? Hell, yes! Preparation is part of your job.

Most guys on a big-league team, like in any collection of human beings, are neither your best friend nor worst enemy, but you still have to be pointed in the same direction to win. How and if the pointing gets done determines how much you win.

Lenny Dykstra, for instance, was bar-none the smartest baseball player I ever played with. Baseball smart, that is. He's the most devoid of common sense of anybody I've ever met. But he had unbelievable baseball savvy. If Lenny said it was a ball, it was a ball. He knew the strike zone better than anybody I ever saw. He just knew how to play.

Yet I honestly believe that Lenny could not concentrate on two things at the same time. When he played, he was hyper-focused on playing baseball. But in any other aspect of life: not so focused.

Now I hear he was a stock guru when the market was bubbling, but he has run into some problems with a magazine and financial services directed to professional athletes. I'm sure he will use the same intelligence and aggressiveness in business that we saw on the field. He can pick one thing in life and just excel at it, almost regardless of what it is. But he can't do two things. Getting guys like Lenny to focus is what it is all about.

Darren Daulton was the guy on those Phillies team that got everyone in harness and kept them there. He is not a born-again Christian. I'm not sure what his religion is, probably more of a New Age type thing, but he believes the world is coming to an end in 2012 and claims he can talk to bugs and lizards. That's his thing. Darren's a friend of mine. I think everybody is entitled to his own beliefs. I don't ever judge anybody by what they believe, but he wasn't that way when we played.

There was an aura around him that he had earned. He had knee surgery but played every day behind the plate. He was the definition of a ballplayer's ballplayer. He could get in someone's face because he was giving everything he had and more. So because of that, he almost never *had* to get into anybody's face.

A lot of times leadership is not some big confrontation or a "Win one for the Gipper" locker room oration. We were playing the Cardinals during the dog days of 1993. We won the first one easily, getting four runs in the first off Joe Magrane and coasting home. I'll never forget the first thing Dutch said when he walked into our clubhouse.

"Nobody say a thing to the papers. Keep this out of the press," Darren said. "We don't want to give them any blackboard stuff. Move on. There's a game tomorrow." I've seen it a hundred times. Players come in all hyped up after a big win, when the game feels easy, and say stuff that just enrages the other team.

Just those few words by Darren helped us keep focused. We did not kick the bear, and wake up the other team. We swept 'em.

It is not unusual for a team leader to be its catcher. That's why so many catchers become managers. Yet it's not just because catchers are the only players on the team who have to relate to both pitchers and position players. I think it's also because catchers have to deal with more pain and physical abuse than any other position.

Some guys have a high tolerance for pain, others do not. It makes a big difference during the course of a season. If you walk out there for a 162 games and you feel pretty good for 60 of them, you've had a pretty healthy season. Fans think that if you're not on the disabled list, you must be okay. Not so. Playing through pain is part of being a professional. Playing through pain so you don't end up hurting yourself even more is tough to do, and you don't always succeed. Catchers naturally need a good attitude toward pain or else they would never put on the gear. That's why a catcher who is a real gamer is such a good example and can become the team leader.

A pitcher, on the other hand, has to be careful. David Cone had stuff that was just filthy. He threw from a lot of different arm angles and all with great velocity. His breaking stuff was amazing, too. I saw him in a day game against Philadelphia when he struck out 19, and he most likely had not turned in early the night before, if you know what I mean. But you figured that a pitcher with that many different arm slots and angles would have arm problems, and he did. But that's what made him a great pitcher.

David is extremely intelligent, was always a leader in the players' union. Joe Torre said that Cone's personality made a great contribution to his Yankees World Series Championship teams. You can have a pitcher whose will to win and overall attitude exerts leadership on a team. But a pitcher can't get into a position-player's face because a starting pitcher is only out there every five days, a reliever only for an inning or two. A pitcher runs the risk of anything he says appearing self-serving, like, "You aren't busing your butt when *I'm* pitching."

Johan Santana got blasted by some media when he criticized a dropped fly ball that cost him a game early in 2009. Rightly so. Those outfielders have to bust their tails for you all season. You don't want to get them mad at you. Let somebody who is out there 162 games be the sheriff.

The season, as it progresses, is a pounding. You need a mind that says, "I don't feel good, but so what." That pitcher doesn't throw to you based on how you feel. Big leaguers hit and pitch to what they see. They see a weakness, they'll keep pounding you on it.

You keep getting pounded, the next thing you know you are in a slump. "Slump," however, is another word that gets used far more by commentators than players. Slumps usually refer to hitting, but there are fielding and pitching slumps, too. Absolutely. It would be simple if slumps were mechanical, and sometimes they are. Mine were all mechanical, until my last couple of years when the desire just wasn't there. If I was struggling, I'd go watch video. I'd watch video every night whether it was good or bad, but I watched even closer when I was bad. I'd find what I needed to fix, except my last year when it just couldn't be fixed anymore.

The trouble is that 90 percent of all slumps are mental. The ability is there, but something's gone wrong from the neck up. Slumps come down to a belief in what you are doing. Sometimes a guy can have a run of bad luck, and he wrongly thinks he's doing something wrong. So he starts to screw around with his mechanics and he *creates* something wrong.

If you're putting the bat on the ball and it goes right at somebody, you can't control that. But if the broadcaster and the press book say you are 4 for your last 25, you will hear the word "slump" associated with your performance, even if you know you've hit three balls that some kangaroo in the outfield went over the fence to catch or three line drives back through the box that pitchers caught by surprise and in self-defense.

That's why Yogi Berra was smart when he said, "I ain't in a slump. I just ain't hittin'." He meant he's been hitting in bad luck, not that his ability to hit has changed or that there is something mechanically wrong.

Yogi Berra's mentor, Bill Dickey, knew this back when he was the Yankees' hitting coach. Slumps haven't changed. He told a reporter in 1960, "A slump is an awful thing. It comes out of nowhere and sticks around until one day it suddenly goes off nowhere. And there is no known cure that works all the time. Talking to a slumping player is just about the worst thing a coach can do. A slump is more mental than physical."

He goes on to say that when Mickey Mantle slumped, it usually *was* physical. His legs were so bad that some games he just couldn't get them to work as well as he needed. Teammate Bill Skowron tended to slump through no fault of his own. A gap hitter back when Yankee Stadium was cavernous, he would hit 380-foot line drives to the alleys and get only outs. Gil McDougald would slump when he tried to pull the ball too much. If the wiry infielder hit a few homers, he would try to hit more and end up with nothing, still a common way to induce a slump for guys who try to hit more homers than they really can.

Pitching slumps work the same way. You can make good pitches, and if a guy drops in a flare and beats you, you can't control that. But sometimes today a guy will just get lit up and still say, "I made some good pitches out there. They just hit them." If a guy breaks his bat and hits a 97 hopper into the hole for a hit, yes, you've still made a good pitch. If somebody rattles your slider around the upper deck, that is not a good pitch.

Of course, that same hitter can swing at the same pitch that got hit a mile and miss next time. It's all about just recognizing what you are doing and being honest with yourself. I threw a lot of pitches that guys would swing through and I'd say, "Holy crap! How did he miss that?" But you don't want to mistake that for a good pitch. You do not want to show that pitch to him again. You do, and you are headed for a slump, which will have nothing to do with your arm and everything to do with your head.

Your head also dictates how your body behaves in between pitches and plays. Whether a player has confidence or doubt is often revealed in his body language. "Body language" is a phrase that you didn't hear around baseball, or anywhere, until it became part of pop psychology in the 1970s. It eventually came into use in sports, and I think it is useful. In fact, coaches have been reading body language forever; there just wasn't a term for it.

Body language in pitchers is enormously important. If you have a look on our face like you are unsure, hitters will pick it up. They don't miss a thing. They can see if you are not confident. Zack Greinke is a perfect case today of great body language. After every pitch he throws, the look on his face shows that he threw it exactly where he wanted. He never gives a hitter anything. Never shakes his head. Nothing.

Hitters will watch the way a pitcher walks to the mound. If that pitcher looks like he hopes he is going to get someone out, those hitters will wear him out. If he looks like he's going to get you out, he will. Mostly.

Carlos Zambrano wears every emotion not only on his sleeve, but on his hat, his glove, and his spikes. You don't have to guess what he's feeling, and that's not a bad thing, unless he starts over-throwing or getting mad, which does not help him. Hey, I love guys who get mad. But if you get mad, you have to be able to use your anger, not allow it to use you. If you get mad and start overthrow-ing and lose your game plan, that's not good. It all depends on how you channel it. There is nothing wrong with emotion on the mound as long as you use it the right way.

Once pitching coaches see a guy walking around, rubbing up the ball after every pitch and generally looking like he's not all that thrilled with the idea of the next one, he will go to the mound. Every pitching coach handles this differently. Sometimes you see a relief pitcher come into the game and he just can't locate at all. Then the coach comes out, talks a minute, and suddenly the guy is a strike machine.

A fan sitting at home thinks, "That's good that he's throwing strikes now, but why in the hell didn't the coach say whatever it was he just told him at the *start* of the inning?"

What gets said varies a lot depending on the coach and the sit-uation. Johnny Podres with the Phillies never said anything about mechanics. I'd walk three guys and all he would say was, "You're throwing good." He never dealt with how bad you were or the trouble you had visited upon yourself. He never said, "You're doing this," or "Don't do that." He either made me laugh by saying some-thing stupid, just to get my mind off my troubles, or he'd pump me up, make me feel good about what I was doing, no matter how bad it was. He never dealt with mechanics. He'd talk about anything but.

From early on, it was always about staying back and staying on top of the ball for me. That's what I had to guard against my whole career. There was not a thing a pitching coach was going to tell me during a game that I didn't know I was doing. If I got to the mound and got wild, I knew why. It was just a matter of being able to correct it.

So that trip to the mound might include telling a joke, or he might be correcting something mechanical. It's more likely to be just, "These guys can't hit you. Turn it loose. Let it go." Sometimes that's all it takes. Pitchers know what they are supposed to do.

The game of baseball is so mental it's not even funny. A pitcher can be sailing along, nobody hitting him, then one guy gets a hit, and they get three or four more in a row. Hitters think, "He got a hit. I can, too." And they do. It's all about confidence.

I read body language of hitters, too. I watched how a guy took a pitch. I had to be able to read bats. If they fouled a pitch, where was the barrel of the bat when he made contact? Can I get the ball by this guy? Is he tentative? Is he going to give up this at-bat, rather than worry about getting hit? I played against guys that would absolutely give up an at-bat. If I threw three strikes, they were going to be out. You can see it. I knew guys that hated to face me and guys who loved to face me. It's just something you learn, if you are paying attention.

Cal Ripken was a guy who never, ever, gave up an at-bat. He was tough to get a book on because he went through about 900 batting stances. Early in my career, I threw about 90 percent fastballs, so with Cal I just tried to stay in on him, because he was a guy who had to get his arms extended. He was going to battle every pitch, and he was another guy it was impossible to intimidate.

You can tell when a guy is giving up. I always watched a hitter's first move. When I was throwing the pitch, if his first move was caving their front side, moving away from the plate, I knew they were thinking of getting hit and not *getting* a hit.

Paul O'Neill made no bones about it. He flat out told me he was scared to death of me. With his first move, his front foot was already heading out of the box when I started toward the plate. He hit a home run off me one day because I messed up and threw the ball inside. So throwing the ball inside to a left-handed hitter isn't always the best strategy, though some people said that's all I did. When a guy just wants to make an easy out by hitting the outside pitch on the ground, let him.

George Brett was probably the most aware guy in baseball when I played. He knew exactly what he was doing every moment he was on the field. The first time he faced me in Arlington, he had never seen me and I had never seen him. Well, I struck him out and the writers came to me after the game and asked me about facing him for the first time and how did I strike him out?

I was just trying to be honest and said something like, "Well, you are talking about a left-handed hitter. I throw hard up and in, so George might not have been real comfortable at-bat against me."

So how do the writers interpret that? They write, "Mitch Williams says that George Brett is afraid of him." George and I laugh about this now, but that is not what I said at all. I said facing a guy who is wild, you might not be real comfortable. Not scared.

So the next time I face George, in Kansas City, he hit his 200th career homer off me, getting his 1,000th run batted in. The next day George is in the paper, quoted as saying, "Yeah, but I was scared while hitting it."

Ozzie Smith was a guy who taught me something. I threw to a lot of power hitters in the American League, and I threw inside fastballs to all of them. All night long, I just lived up in the zone, getting them to chase. When I moved to the National League, I threw Ozzie Smith that high fastball and he almost took my head off.

It only took one more rocket back through the box for me to figure out he was not the kind of hitter who would chase my heater, looking to put it in the upper deck. He was just looking to put the bat on the ball. He was not going to be long with his swing. From then on, I threw Ozzie nothing but breaking balls, and he never got another hit off me.

Darryl Strawberry had a hard time even making contact on me. He was a guy with amazing power, but he had a huge hole in his swing. Because of the way he stood in against me, his hands always looked like a target to me. If I could get the ball at his hands, he could not catch up. If you left it out over the plate, or down, he'd kill it. He was 0-for-life against me. So you never know which hitter is going to be a tough matchup for which pitcher. Greg Maddux said the toughest hitter for him was Mickey Morandini!

One thing that doesn't matter to players very much, most of the time, is where they are playing. Everyone prefers home cooking, but the road is pretty much the road. It didn't matter to me whether a park was a so-called hitter's park or pitcher's park. Any pitcher who says he doesn't like to pitch in a particular park is worried about the wrong thing. If you make pitches, you get people out. If you make mistakes, they will hit it out of Yosemite.

I didn't like the Astrodome, Seattle, Minnesota, or any place that had a dome. I believe baseball is an outdoor game. The only place I hated to go was Montreal. It was pitiful how quiet that place was. I didn't care where I was as long as it was loud and I could get some adrenaline pumping. I didn't care if they were booing me or cheering me, either one got me going.

The exception was Minnesota. That was the loudest place I've ever been in my life. It's the only place in baseball where the home field is a real advantage. When they get a full house in that place, you can't hear your catcher talking to you when you are both on the mound. Throw in the fact that fielders can't see balls hit in the air because of the gray ceiling and the baggies in the outfield that give weird caroms, and you have a place that is, shall we say, unique. By the time a visiting team gets used to all this, they're gone.

Who knows what the team's new outdoor stadium will do to this home-field advantage the team has enjoyed for so long? I can understand that Twins fans will love being outside on nice summer evenings after enduring those winters. I do wonder what April baseball will be like, since the season starts at least a week earlier than it did the last time the Twins played outdoors. You would think the person or the computer that makes up the schedule would take this into consideration and maybe have the Twins start the season on the road. That may be too logical, and maybe it's another kind of unfair to have to start on the road every year.

While most players don't allow fan reaction to affect their play, they are aware that fans are pretty different from city to city. Players certainly felt the rivalry between the Phillies and Mets, even in years when either or both teams might not have been that good. It wasn't that players got more "up" for the Mets. You have to be "up" every night. But you are aware that you are playing the Mets, and that means something. You didn't want to lose to them. Ever.

I got yelled at nonstop at Shea. That's the way it's supposed to be. If you walked into Shea not wearing a Mets uniform, you got bombarded. There isn't any difference between Mets and Yankees fans in this regard. Hey, that's a compliment.

If you saw the parade in Philadelphia after the 2008 World Series, you saw that there is not a city anywhere that backs its teams better. One thing you can always count on from Philadelphia fans is honesty. You can be the best player on the planet, and if you have a bad day in Philadelphia, the fans are going to let you know it. I've said it from the minute I came here—these fans do not boo a player, they boo a performance. I've never had a problem with that.

As soon as you recognize, as a player, that you sucked today, be the first one to say, "I sucked today." Then what are the fans going to do with that? "The guy already said he sucked," they'll say. And that will be the end of the story. It's the guys who come out and say, "I didn't get this call," or "I caught a bad break," that Philadelphia fans really get on. You did *not* get a bad break. There are no bad breaks. You either have it or you don't, you get it done or you don't, and if you don't get it done one night, say so, forget about it, and go back out the next night and get it done.

If Ryan Howard hit two home runs yesterday, they will have cheered him. If he strikes out three times today, they will boo him. Ask Mike Schmidt.

Cubs fans are great, too. I give credit to them. They show up. When their team does well, there is no fan base that is happier. I give credit to fans in any city that show up. I have respect for that city.

To me, Tampa in 2008 was appalling. You had these young kids out there, who played their asses off all year long, and the night before they clinch the AL East, they had 17,000 people there. That's an atrocity.

Rangers fans are football fans. In certain parts of the country, football is the only thing, and Texas in one of those places. There was a lack of baseball knowledge among the Rangers fans when I played there. Texas is my favorite state in the whole country, I love it, but there's not a lot of passion for baseball. The only way they are ever going to draw fans is if they win. That's it. Winning cures a lot of ills, and they have never managed it. It seems they have never had an owner who combined deep pockets with knowing what it takes to win, like a George Steinbrenner. They have sometimes had one or the other, but never both.

Cardinals fans are good baseball fans. In fact, everywhere in the Midwest, fans are great: Kansas City, Milwaukee. They are going to show up regardless. You can have a bad team, and they will still come. That's just the way they were raised. They believe, "Look. We live in St. Louis. We go to Cardinals games." That's all there is to it.

They are not as rabid as fans in the East. They don't boo as much; don't act out as much; don't yell at players as much. That's just a reflection of the difference in lifestyle between the Midwest and the East.

On the East Coast, the fans live for it. It's their escape. For them, it's all sports, not just baseball. There is not as much to do in the Midwest, so a larger percentage of people there are fans, maybe, but they are more laid back about it. They may be passionate, but their passion is more contained.

By the time you get to the West Coast, attending baseball is not life or death like back East, nor is it part of everybody's daily life, like the Midwest. It's a social event. A perfect illustration of the fans out West is Kirk Gibson's famous walk-off homer versus Dennis Eckersley. The next time you see a video of that, watch as he's circling the bases. Look through the right-field bleachers at all the taillights leaving the parking lot. They get there in the second inning and leave in the seventh.

There are a lot of things to do in Los Angeles or San Diego. Places like that don't need another distraction. In Philadelphia and New York, people need the distraction. Those are stressful cities to live. In Philadelphia, especially, people bust their asses five–six days a week, 10–12 hours a day. You can bet they don't want any excuses from professional athletes. Nor should there be any.

Chapter Four

Phillies, Phriends, and Phoes

When I started working on this book, I had no idea I would be spending the summer of 2008 watching every game of the eventual World Champions. As I write this now, I have no idea if I will have watched back-to-back World Championship teams, but I got a helluva shot at it. These Phillies teams have been special—not only rewarding long-suffering Philadelphia fans, but also showing all of baseball what outstanding players they have and how they fit together to make an outstanding team. Believe me, it is very, very possible to have the first but not the second.

I was in spring training for a couple of days with the Phillies in 2008. My first impression was that the offense would be fine. If the pitching could keep the other side under six runs a game, the team might do all right. There were huge questions in both the starting rotation and the bullpen. Of course, just about every question mark turned into an exclamation point.

The team started out slowly, as usual, barely exceeding .500 by May 1. I don't think they are a hot weather team, but who is? It seems to me every year the schedule is made up by somebody who thinks every game is played in Palm Springs. Why not have the cold weather teams on the road a little bit more in April and at home a little bit more in July?

A few players are made for cold weather, but most of them aren't. Ryan Howard is a terrible cold-weather player. Put him in a dome, and there's no telling what kind of numbers he might put up. As it is, even at his young age, people are ready to say he's finished because of his slow starts. But when the weather gets hot, so does Ryan, and so far the cold weather in September and October doesn't seem to bother him. Good thing for the Phillies.

Chase Utley was unbelievable in April and May. He doesn't care what the weather does, he just wants to play. He's a warm-weather guy from California, but it wouldn't matter to him if there were 6 inches of snow on the infield. From the neck up, he's as strong as I've ever seen. When it's cold in April, hitters don't want to get jammed because they know it's going to hurt. There are guys that let that affect them. Chase doesn't. He doesn't let anything affect his play.

In the second half of 2008, Utley had a serious hip problem. He wouldn't tell anyone. Obviously, the Phillies knew internally, but he didn't want it to get out. He didn't want anybody to know. He knew the team needed him. He just went out and played. If you saw him struggle during the season, it was because of his hip. He never went on the DL.

A player's ability to play through injuries is all mind over matter. If you don't mind, it don't matter.

Sparky Anderson once said, "Pain don't hurt." He meant that a lot of injuries, aches, and pains that everyone gets during a season don't have to bother your level of play.

If you don't tell anybody, nobody is going to know. Utley didn't want anybody to know that he might possibly have a weakness. He just went out and played through the pain. More players do that than you might think. I went out and played basically my whole career with a bad knee.

The time to get concerned is when an injury becomes apparent on the field. There are too many guys now, signed to long contracts, who don't have to be worried about being "Wally Pipped." Pipp got a headache, asked out of the Yankees lineup, and never got back in. Having Lou Gehrig as your backup is a bad career move. Now if guys get a little sore, they don't know the difference between injured and sore. There are guys who truly can't play because of injury. I understand that. The guys I have trouble with say, "I'm a little stiff today. I can't play."

I remember Chris Brown when he was in San Diego. He's the guy who took himself out of the lineup because he said he slept on his eye wrong. Those are the guys I have zero respect for.

If a pitcher told Tom House he didn't feel good, Tom would say, "Well, a hitter doesn't hit how you feel."

If you don't show him you don't feel good, he's not going to know.

Jamie Moyer looks like he doesn't feel good every start. That's not always a bad sign. Roberto Clemente had chronic back problems and complained constantly. It got so that the more he complained, the better his teammates felt about it. They came to recognize that if Roberto said he felt terrible, there was a good chance he'd get three or four hits. When his back was yipping, he'd swing a little less violently and make more contact.

Jim Palmer and Earl Weaver argued forever about whether or not Palmer's aches and pains were in his arm or his head. I think it was Palmer who said, "Those psychosomatic injuries are tough to overcome." I think it was Palmer because I don't see Weaver using a word like "psychosomatic."

In the days before long contracts, players were afraid to take a day off. There were 10 guys waiting to take their jobs. Today it isn't always the players who ask for time off. The teams want to protect their investments. That's what pitch counts are all about.

House always believed in what I could do. He always thought he could fix me up enough to get me to the major leagues and keep me there. Without someone in your corner with that kind of dedication and faith, a lot of us would have been sent home early—like Ryan Madson.

Madson looked like he was beginning to put it all together toward the end of 2007. When it became apparent early in 2008 that his improvement was going to continue, it was a huge boost to the team. It was like a light bulb went on in his head.

Ryan throws a fastball, cutter, and change. I told him he was guiding his changeup. I told him that if he didn't believe in it, nobody else would. If you're going to throw it, you have to *throw* it.

He was also a guy whose makeup I questioned earlier in his career. It was all facial expression with him. He looked like he was beat when he walked through the outfield fence.

Then at the end of 2007, and continuing through all of the next year, things sort of clicked for him. It was like he said to himself, "Hey, I can be pretty good!" When you walk onto that mound, if you don't believe you can get it done, there isn't a soul in that ballpark who's going to believe it.

"Guiding your changeup" means that you could see his arm slowing down. There cannot be any difference in your mechanics and delivery between your fastball and change. Hitters swing at arm speed; they are not swinging at the ball. If they waited to see the ball, they'd never get the bat off their shoulders.

That's why Santana and Hamels have such unbelievable changeups. You can almost put Madson's in that class now. When

Ryan Madson pitched against the Washington Nationals on April 27, 2009, in Philadelphia. (AP Images)

you throw it, you have to trust that your grip is going to do what you need it to do. That's why it's so tough to learn the pitch— because your natural instinct is to change your arm speed. When you get to the point of trusting your grip and can just let it go, then you have hitters swinging at arm speed and hitting nothing but air.

It's a way of trusting your stuff. I couldn't do it. Few pitchers do. Hitters are always looking for something in your delivery to tip a pitch, whatever it may be. Show them a slower arm motion so they can read "changeup," and they will hit that ball a considerable distance.

I threw a splitter. It was all right. I didn't use it a lot, but it fit my mindset better than a change. I was a power pitcher. I wanted to throw everything as hard as I could. When my splitter worked, it worked. When it didn't, it got hit a long way. It's a little slower than a fastball, but it's the movement that's important. If it doesn't drop, it becomes just a very hittable fastball.

It was the "in" pitch of the 1980s, but not so much now. I think some people were trying to attribute a lot of arm injuries to it. I don't see anything about a splitter that would contribute to arm injuries. You can look at guys like Schilling and Clemens. It absolutely made a difference in their careers. If they don't have the split, they don't win nearly as many games. Jack Morris had a helluva splitter, too.

You have to get on top of it. If you get under it come at it from the side, it's nothing. It's flat. You have to get on top for it to go down. I used to sit around stretching my fingers to prepare for the splitter.

Cutters, or cut fastballs, have sort of become the vogue pitch now. When I pitched, there was a slider or a fastball; you didn't hear about cutters. I think of Greg Maddux as being the guy who launched that pitch. He knew he could throw that sinker at a

Greg Maddux pitched in what would become his 327th career victory on July 29, 2006. (AP Images)

left-hander's hip and it would run back and catch the inside of the plate. Batters began to realize what was happening to them, and they started thinking, "We gotta trust that that pitch is going to come back over the plate."

So he started cutting it on them. Instead of going back over the plate, it cut in further. He was blowing out bats left and right. All you need to do is change the position of your fingers on the seams. It is a very small adjustment, and Maddux was a surgeon.

Mariano Rivera's cutter is a natural. I'm not sure he can throw a ball straight. He threw a cutter to second base for an error in the ninth inning of the final game of the 2001 World Series. I don't know of anybody who has broken the bats of more lefties than Mariano.

Andy Pettitte uses it well, too. It lets a lefty who doesn't throw all that hard have a way to go inside to righties.

That's a main difference in the game today. Nobody wants to go in there. I think most of it is not that pitchers are afraid of making a mistake inside and getting into the batter's wheelhouse instead of his kitchen, but rather that the game is just different today.

We see warnings issued in the first innings on pitches that didn't even hit anybody. To me, that ruins the game. What people have to understand is that a pitcher is standing 60 feet from a swinging bat. If a hitter doesn't have some fear of that baseball, they are going to hit and somebody is going to get hurt.

At one point in the 1950s, Branch Rickey made the Pittsburgh Pirate pitchers wear batting helmets on the mound in spring training. Of course, they hated it. It is weird, if you have ever seen any photos of those guys back then, to see Nellie King or Bob Friend with a helmet on while pitching. But I understand the thinking. I have a bump on my head that I got in 1989 that will never go away, thanks to a low line drive.

There has to be some hesitation on the hitter's part when he steps into the box. He needs to think there might be some price to pay for hanging out and diving over the plate. That's how the game has changed—when you start seeing balls hit out of right field at will by righty hitters. Maybe it's been the use of steroids by some that caused this, but it's also because hitters can dive without fear.

Derek Jeter is the poster child for guys who dive across the plate. But at least he never squawks the few times he gets plunked for it. He is an absolute inside-out hitter. To me, you get him out by throwing him away. Let him hit flies to right, or singles; nothing that's going to hurt you. You leave a ball in the middle of the plate with him diving, and now he can drive the ball to right,

Yankees shortstop Derek Jeter was hit by a pitch during the 2009 All-Star Game in St. Louis. (AP Images)

or hook it. The only way Jeter's going to drive the inside pitch is if it's a breaking ball or something off-speed.

Manny Ramirez has been the best right-handed hitter alive for a few years because he stays inside the fastball no matter what. You want to get him out, you have to come way in first, then go away. But it's hard to go that far inside because he's got unbelievable hands and he trusts his hands. He's confident he can fight anything off inside, not only fight it off but more often than not hit it hard somewhere. There is nothing for him to fear because if you pitch inside, the umpire will throw you out of the game.

In the playoffs once, a pitch went behind his head, and Manny got pissed. Tough. You have to be smart enough to know when a guy is throwing at you and when a pitcher just lost his grip and the ball sailed.

Watch Ramirez closely when he walks. Sometimes he hesitates before he starts toward first. I've heard it's because when he's at bat, he doesn't keep track of the balls, just the strikes. That's relaxed.

So like I said, Madson came out with more confidence. The entire game of baseball is built on confidence. If you are not confident, the hitters will smell it. You could see him during the 2008 season get more and more sure of himself and his ability.

Chad Durbin was another guy who helped a lot. When he came over from Detroit, he was vying for the fifth starter's job. He went to the bullpen and still had questions about if he wanted to start.

It's a matter of his thinking, "I've been a starter all my life. I don't know if I can relieve, or if I want to." Did he get tired toward the end of the year? Yeah, he did. I'm sure he's prepared for it now.

He was another guy who came out and had some success early, got confidence, which led to more success, and it just snowballed.

Believe me, when some guys come out of the pen, the hitter's say, "I can't wait until this guy gets into the game."

I've watched it. Mike Williams was a mop-up guy here in '93. Later he had one year in the regular rotation, but only one. He did not have anything. Then he went to Pittsburgh, saved a couple of games, and they made him their closer. That changed everybody's perception of him. Now he comes in and, "Oh, shit. The closer's in the game." It's the same Mike Williams that used to mop up. But he's got a new moniker. He's the closer. It all has to do with perception.

Madson used to be the guy that the other teams couldn't wait to get into the game. Now it's, "Damn. Madson's in."

Durbin replaced Kenny Rogers in the Tigers' rotation in 2007. The first time around the league, he was okay. Then the league caught up with him. The same thing happened to him in Kansas City and Cleveland. As a starter, he doesn't have anything to make a hitter have to adjust after facing him the first time at bat. As a reliever, they only get to see him once. The next time, it's Madson.

That's why I couldn't start. The fastball quit tricking them after one time through the order. I was not a big control guy, to say the least. For my career, I gave up more walks than hits. Not many, if *any*, can say that, or would necessarily want to. I mean, I knew every hitter's "nitro zone," but I wasn't going out and painting the corners. Every hitter has a nitro zone. My job was to know where it was and to stay away from it. Everybody knew I was going to throw a fastball, but a hitter cannot guard the whole plate.

When I came over to Philadelphia from Chicago, the first pitcher's meeting I sat in on, they said, "We can't get Dawson and Sandberg out." I told them, "Stay away!"

All you have to do is throw the ball on the outside corner of the plate, and they are not going to hurt you. Same as Jeter, but for a different reason. They were playing in Wrigley Field, and their first movement was to cheat to get to the ball inside, so they can hit it over the left field fence. They would never hit a homer to right. It's simple. You have to watch a hitter. You have to watch his plan of attack. Will they hit a single to right? Yes. But they are not going to hit the ball out of the park to right.

That's all I cared about. I wanted to stay away from a hitter's happy zone. Where is his power?

Part of the success of the 2008 Phillies was that several guys found their identities as big leaguers. For Durbin, it was as a reliever. I thought the first time I saw him he could fit in great as a one- or two-inning guy.

Likewise with Greg Dobbs, who was the best pinch-hitter in baseball in 2008. If you play him every day, he'll get completely overexposed. Pitchers find a way to go at him, and you don't want that. Charlie Manuel helped him find his identity, and Dobbs is wearing a championship ring today.

Dobbs is like Lenny Harris; he doesn't play every day. There is a point in your career where you have to accept that. Harris was not that good defensively, nor did he hit with enough power to play every day. But he could sit on the bench for three hours and then hit a single when you needed it most.

This is how team success is based on the success of individuals. Because the other starters did okay, Durbin did not have to start. He found that his one or two innings were as important to winning as the first six.

Just about everybody in the majors and the minors was a superstar in high school or college. They all thought they could be stars in the majors, too. They can't. Some adapt. Others don't. But you *can* be super at the job you are given to do.

Speaking of confidence and accepting your role, watching Cole Hamels emerge from a fine young pitcher with potential into a front-of-the-rotation starter has been interesting. He just began figuring out, "Oh. I can be that guy who throws 220–230 innings. I can be a No. 1." But he didn't become that until the playoffs in 2008.

To me, Jamie Moyer was the ace all through the regular season in 2008. That has to do strictly with leadership. When guys got behind Jamie, they thought they were going to win. The hitters knew they were going to be in the ball game. They knew they didn't have to score 10 runs that day. The young pitchers see somebody who looks like he's throwing batting practice, and he's winning. They think, "I better pay attention. I might learn something."

Jamie doesn't lead just by what he does on the mound, either. He is able to get his points across by talking to the kids. They don't look at him and say, "Look old man. Just leave me alone." He will offer help, and you are only stupid if you don't listen.

You are not going to do everything the way Jamie Moyer does because you are not the same pitcher. You have to be smart enough to know there is something that is going to come out of his mouth that can benefit you.

Some guys don't pay enough attention. I spent my whole career trying to just recognize what was happening. Is this hitter on me, ahead of me, or behind me?

There are pitchers who will throw a fastball that the hitter is so far behind it's pitiful, and the next pitch will be a changeup. Why? Why would you want to speed up a guy's bat? If you can learn from someone like Moyer, you don't have to learn the hard way by watching your changeup lined into the lower deck.

Hamels' mechanics are pretty consistent. But he's learning to make adjustments during the game. If your breaking ball isn't good that day, you have to adjust.

Some hitters are pretty smart, too. My last week in the big leagues in Kansas City, I struck out Bernie Williams with a splitter. In

121

Jamie Moyer is a leader on the mound and in the bullpen. (AP Images)

my last game in the big leagues, I got ahead of him with two strikes. I threw him a split, and he hit it into the left-field bleachers.

Some adjustments need to be made from season to season, some from week to week, others during a game. The guys who can adjust *during* a game have the most success.

For instance, Hamels only has a get-it-over-the-plate curve right now. If I'm Hamels, I don't throw it unless it's the first pitch or I'm behind on the count. If he tries to get guys out with it, they pummel it. It doesn't have that bite going down or away that a get-me-out curveball has. Brett Myers has one of those.

There is a recognition factor for hitters, looking for fastballs early on the count. If they see a curve, they are going to take it, because no hitter wants to hit a breaking ball on the first pitch. So Cole throws his just-okay curve for a strike early and plants the image in the hitter's mind: "He might throw me another curve." And if I'm Cole, I never go back to that. The key is being able to throw it for a strike, not how backbreaking it is.

Nobody elected or appointed Jamie Moyer leader of the pitching staff. Nobody told Hamels he was looked upon as the new one. Leadership of a pitching staff is a presumptive thing. It's how the guys view you.

It takes more than two starters, of course. Brett Myers showed me something in 2008. He stunk. He was terrible. He's a hardheaded guy, but he took an assignment to the minors and did what he needed to do to come back and have success. Not every guy under a big-league contract would say, "Yeah. I'll go back to the minors."

Adam Eaton was another guy making millions of dollars, and he didn't go down and work on anything. He just left. He hasn't changed a thing. He's happy with the money he's going to put in the bank, and you'll never hear from him again. In fact, the Phillies released him early in spring training of 2009, eating a huge hunk of money in the process.

The Orioles signed Eaton for 2009 and gave him eight starts. He went 2-5 with an 8.56 earned run average. Released again.

The Rockies signed Eaton to a minor-league contract and brought him up in August to bolster their bullpen. He pitched just like he had in Baltimore and ended up back in the minors.

I don't know Adam. He might be a great guy. All I can do is comment on what I see on the field. For him to be successful, all he has to do is get on top of the ball. If you are not smart enough to go in and watch video and see that yourself, then you are not working hard enough at your craft.

You can't go out and get pounded one game, then have good stuff the next, and not see the difference on video. It's simple. When he's around the baseball gets hammered. When he throws the ball downhill, he's got good stuff. That's how easy the adjustment would be for him, but he doesn't make it. Why?

It's easy to point out. It's a mystery of the game why one guy makes an adjustment and another doesn't. It's easy to diagnose the disease and hard to find the cure.

When Todd Benzinger came up with the Red Sox during the 1987 season, he had been tearing up Triple A. But he started out in Boston very slowly. Then he got hot. People wanted to know why he had struggled and what he had changed.

He said he had been waiting for mistakes to hit, like he did in Triple A. But pitchers in the majors just didn't make mistakes as often or as badly. He finally decided that he had to start swinging at tougher pitches if he was ever going to get his bat off his shoulder. He lasted nine years in the big leagues. He was never a superstar, but he survived. Adjustments.

When the Phillies picked up Joe Blanton late in 2008, nobody was very excited about it. But what impressed me about the kid is that he stays healthy and takes the ball. He's not going to overly impress you with his stuff, but when you look him up, he went 4–0 in 13 starts. He keeps his team in the game better than a guy with great stuff that he can't command.

That's all they really need from him. He's a perfect fourth or fifth starter. He's not a guy you give a top spot in your rotation to, but those starts by the back end of your rotation count, too. And you are not counting on them as wins. In those games, you are just looking to see that in the fifth inning, you are still in the game.

To some people, Brad Lidge's 2008 was a big surprise. Not to me. We talked about it at the end of 2007. He was struggling, and I did an interview for a show in Philadelphia. They asked me if I had the chance to go get Brad Lidge, would I? I said yes without question. You don't find that kind of arm every day.

When Lidge was in Houston, he had gotten away from doing some important things. When a hitter is at the plate, you have to make him move his feet and change his eye level. If all he has to do is look down, I don't care how good your stuff is, he is going to hit it. You have to make him look up, down, and up again. If he doesn't have to change his eye level and only has to look down, you have made it too easy on him.

Phillies closer Brad Lidge throws three different sliders. (AP Images)

In Houston, everything that Lidge threw was down. Now he has three different sliders: a get-me-over one, then he's got another one that breaks a lot more, kind of like a slurve, and then he's also got that punch-out slider that just disappears.

But, if he throws his fastball down, too, in the same plane as the slider, then his slider becomes much more hittable. When he's throwing his fastball from the belt to right under the chin, now the hitter can't look in just one location: down. Now the hitter has to be alert. The pitcher might straighten you up. And if a hitter has to worry about being straightened up, it takes away a lot from his diving out and over the plate. That's what Lidge got back to in 2008, and he was as good a closer as I'd ever seen. You can't be better than perfect, which is what he was. He blew exactly zero saves the whole year!

You also need guys at the end of your staff to be useful, too. Rudy Seanez was like that in 2008. He has always been serviceable. He was a guy who threw extremely hard early in his career, and later he had to start mixing in breaking balls. But he's always done the job and been more than adequate. He won't just keep getting knocked around, like some guys do who are fighting for that last spot on the staff. He's always been able to make the adjustments necessary to make himself stay viable.

He got his first ring with the Phillies after 17 years in the majors. Yet he still got released as part of the numbers game, the consequence of playing for a good team with lots of young arms. The Angels signed him to a minor-league contract in May 2009 and, after indifferent results, released him two months later. So maybe Rudy is finally retired. Don't bet on it. Not with his desire and the shape of a lot of big-league bullpens. Some guys survive, and some don't.

Look at a list of the 100 best prospects from five years ago, and you won't even recognize 60 of the names. Somebody else who was a 30th-round draft choice will be on the All-Star team—like John Kruk. He got $500 and a bus ticket to sign. Some people see things in a player right away that most people don't.

One thing about baseball: put a guy out there long enough, and you are going to find out about him. You get players coming out of high school who played maybe 40 games last year. You see athletic ability, but you don't know what they are going to do over a 120-game minor-league season, much less 162. They weed each other out.

It's not just athletic ability. It's ability *plus* the mental toughness required to do it every day. Utley played through his hip injury because he knew his team needed him in the lineup. If I'm building a team, he's the first guy I want.

I'd want Jimmy Rollins, too, of course. Best all-around shortstop in baseball. When he said, "We are the team to beat," he caught a lot of flack, but he was proven correct. It isn't bragging if it's true. I don't think he was arrogant. He went out and won the MVP. He has a way of firing up the other guys, getting the most out of them.

Speaking of fire, remember Bobby Abreu on the Phillies? In Philadelphia, he was a guy often accused of lacking fire. Same when he went to the Yankees. The trouble is, here in Philadelphia, for quite a few years, he was "the guy," and I don't think that's a good role for him. I don't think he's an East Coast kind of guy. I think the East Coast is way too volatile, too excitable, and Bobby Abreu is not an excitable guy.

Now he's with the Angels and just one of a whole lineup that's hitting about .300. He's having another Bobby Abreu year after a lot of people wrote him off. He is more appreciated in a place where the people who show up are not rabid fans, where it's more of a social event than a way of life.

He does everything so easily, people think he's loafing. He's not a guy who is going to run into an outfield wall. Bobby has always thought the wall had teeth. But he's a guy who makes plays. And he's a great hitter. It just doesn't look like he's trying that hard, and on the East Coast, fans don't like that.

Early in 2009, Bobby helped beat Justin Verlander with a walk in the first inning. He just refused to swing at anything but a strike. A few batters later, Morales hit a three-run homer off a fastball at 3–2. Why? Because Bobby had shown, for that inning at least, that Verlander could not throw anything but a fastball for a strike. Getting that walk showed more baseball ability, or more precisely baseball intelligence, than hitting the homer.

A fan doesn't know the person. A fan can't see inside as easily as a teammate. A lot of my friends are bull riders. Some riders get on a bull, ride him, make the 8-second whistle, and get off. You watch them and say, "He's not even trying." They make it look so dead easy it looks like no effort is going into it.

Then you get another rider who gets the crowd on its feet. He's hanging off the side of the bull and it looks like he's giving everything he has just to hang on. It's the same 8 seconds. It doesn't make one rider better than the other. The one guy just makes it look easier. That's Abreu. It's like they said about Johnny Cash's music—just because it's simple don't mean it's easy. Abreu makes it look easy, but that doesn't mean he's not trying or giving everything he's got.

You look at a duck swimming on a pond. From above the water, it doesn't look like he's doing anything. But under water, he's working his ass off.

Speaking of guys the Philadelphia fans didn't warm up to, when the Phillies let Pat Burrell walk, I thought it was a mistake. Turns out it wasn't, but I was still glad that Pat stayed around long enough to earn a ring. It takes a special kind of guy to play in Philadelphia. This is a guy who listened to as much bad stuff said about him as anyone who has ever come through this town. He never whined, never complained. He just went out and played. Not to mention he was a right-handed hitter in a very left-handed lineup. For 2009, they added a lefty bat, Raul Ibanez, who is four years older and is not even an upgrade in the outfield.

Tampa went out and did what I thought the Phillies should have done. They went out and got Pat because they are a very lefty lineup. Keeping Burrell would have also given them a guy they know will react well if things go wrong.

Neither guy can run. Pat throws better. One thing about Burrell, and I've sung his praises about this for years: he does everything fundamentally right. He can't run at all. He's not going to make any diving catches in the gap. But he can go out and make the routine play and throw to the right base and hit the cutoff man. This is not appreciated enough by fans, nor pointed out enough by commentators, but the players and coaches know.

Bo Jackson was one of the best athletes who ever lived, let alone play in the big leagues. He could make amazing catches, outrun the ball, and hit it 9 miles. Birdie Tebbetts, who was in baseball from the Babe to Bo, said that Ruth's bat was the only one he ever heard with the same "crack" that Bo's had. But for every highlight film you could make of him, if you watched him every day, you could also make a much longer lowlight film. He just didn't have much experience playing baseball.

I watched Bo play when I pitched. He had a lot of holes in his swing. If I was on the mound, I'd trade those occasional diving catches in the gap or leaping ones at the wall over the course of a season for the guy who hits the cutoff man every time and throws to the right base.

Speaking of baseball smarts, I love Shane Victorino. He's a guy who plays as hard as he can play every play. He isn't going to build you a rocket anytime soon, but he'll be the first one to climb on board. He is not the most savvy baseball mind in the world. He tried to steal third with two outs and Burrell at the plate one time and got thrown out. You just can't make those kinds of mistakes.

But Charlie Manuel was smart, as usual. He moved him down to the sixth hole, which basically allowed him to be an athlete. When he was hitting second, it wasn't the best fit. Hitting second, there is a lot going on besides just hitting. You have to know if your job is to move the runner, if you have to take a pitch to let a runner steal, or if you need to hit behind the runner. That's not Shane's game.

If Shane wants to steal third with two outs and the No. 8 hitter up, what are you going to say? He's trying to make something happen. But if you do it with the No. 5 hitter up, a guy who is paid to drive in runs, then you look stupid.

Shane's baseball IQ gradually improved, and in 2009 he hit second most of the time and made the All-Star Team, to boot. He's a great outfielder, and he still has not reached his potential as a hitter. He doesn't get the attention he deserves.

Of course, not everybody on a team is a great athlete. Or, at least, not everybody looks like one. Matt Stairs looks like your plumber. But he is one of those guys you want to root for, whether you are a fan or an ex-player. He's a flat-out professional hitter. When he came up to bat in the 2008 playoffs against Jonathan Broxton, who has a great fastball, I said, "If he gets that fastball down, watch out. Matt can hit any fastball ever thrown." And you saw what happened.

That's why the Phillies got him. He's a left-handed bat, and if you bring a hard-throwing righty closer in the game, he can hit the ball over the fence. You are not going to find a lot of places in the field for him, and he doesn't care. The great thing about Matt is he understands his role and embraces it. He says to himself, "I know I can hit any fastball that comes over, and that's what I'm gonna try and do." He makes no bones about it. And he will *not* get

Shane Victorino races around first on a sixth-inning triple in Game 4 of the NLCS on Monday, October 19, 2009, in Philadelphia.

cheated. He says that with every swing he takes in batting practice, he is trying to hit the ball out of the park. He's a guy who knows what he's there for.

You don't have to have a big bat to have an impact. Pedro Feliz's contribution to winning the championship is overlooked because it came from his glove. I had no idea he was that good at third. Talk about somebody who makes it look easy! I watched him through 162 games in 2008. I don't think I saw him make a single bad throw. Seems like every one he made was chest high, right where it's supposed to be.

You do not need an All-Star at every position. You need players who do what needs to be done. The Phillies needed solid defense at third more than they needed offense. Pedro helped the Phillies more than a Troy Glaus would have. If you can't hide a bat in the Phillies lineup, there's trouble. He should not have any pressure put on him to hit. If he hits, that's a bonus. When you have Jaime Moyer on your staff, who throws a lot of changeups, and you are setting up right-handed hitters to pull the ball, a Pedro Feliz at third is invaluable.

You don't need to score 900 runs unless you are going to let in 899. You can't have a questionable pitching staff *and* a questionable defense. Both have to perform if you are going all the way. I agree with Bill James, the ultimate numbers freak, when he states that a lot of what we think of as good pitching is really good defense. You see a pitcher who one year gives up a lot more hits, walks more, gives up more runs. It might be because the defense behind him has deteriorated: more balls falling in or bouncing through. He might have to pitch more carefully and walk more guys.

Casey Stengel had a bunch of pitchers in the 1950s who never had good years before or after they left the Yankees. It wasn't just the offense carrying them because they didn't have big earned run averages or bad numbers. It wasn't like they were winning every game 9–8. They were known as the Bombers, but their defense was habitually awesome. You can't win just with big bats, not year after year.

Phillies General Manager Pat Gillick is gone now, but he got a lot of credit—and rightly so—for bringing in players like Feliz, Stairs, and Durbin. He was never around very much. He wasn't really visible. He did not make a lot of blockbuster deals, and the ones he did, like getting Adam Eaton, didn't work out that well. What he was great at was making the very quiet deal, which looks insignificant but ends up being huge. When you look at guys like Greg Dobbs and Jayson Werth, these moves look like nothing on the surface. It's like playing chess, and you get a pawn ahead early. It makes a big difference in the end game. How big was Stairs' homer in the 2008 playoffs?

I think Ruben Amaro Jr. will do a good job. He's an intelligent guy. He's been around the game his whole life. He knows baseball and learned under Gillick.

After the weather warmed in 2008, up the team started hitting its stride. There are always a couple of games that are emblematic of the whole season. Late in July, Hamels gave up nine runs in the fourth inning to Atlanta. Coles and Chase both made errors. Teixeira had a single and a homer in that one inning. The Phillies came back with seven in the fifth and won 10–9. That would have been an easy game to lose. You just pack it in and say, "That was a fluke. We'll get 'em tomorrow." But no, they hung in there and won. That's the kind of game pennant winners win.

Later in the season, Victorino threw out a runner at the plate versus Atlanta to preserve a win. Look back over the season and see where these little things mean everything.

Still, the Phillies had a good year, but if the Mets' bullpen had not collapsed, it might have been a whole different season.

Offensively, the Mets played well enough to win. The Phillies didn't play well against them. But you can't blow 27 saves!

There weren't a lot of people around here feeling sorry for former Phillies and Mets closer Billy Wagner when he got hurt. He left a bad taste in a lot of mouths here. Billy had no idea how to play in this town. The way to play in Philadelphia is to keep your mouth shut when things go wrong and just say, "I had a bad night." Billy always wanted to defend himself. You cannot defend yourself here.

Wagner is too vocal for a pitcher. I don't think pitchers should talk about the day-to-day happenings on a team. I don't think a pitcher can be a leader of a team. It has to be a position player. If the media wants a quote, let them get it from somebody who's out there busting his butt every day.

Speaking of busting your butt every day, one thing I would love to see changed on the Mets is the way Jose Reyes carries himself. Maybe next year, coming back from injuries, he will be different. He has a ton of talent. I would love to see him look to his right and see how to work day in and day out.

For me, David Wright is one of the best examples today of how to play the game. He's an outstanding player. For a few years now, the Mets have had four All-Star position players surrounded by a group of marginal major leaguers, either past their prime or not yet in it. Even when they do have their studs in the lineup, they don't play together.

Willie Randolph was the scapegoat for a bunch of guys who didn't go out there and perform the way they were supposed to. I don't know why that was Willie's fault, or why it is Jerry Manuel's—who has faced the exact same thing, plus a ridiculous number of injuries. What they need on the Mets is somebody to put his thumb on the throats of these players and say, "This is the way it's going to be done." But I don't know if you can even manage that way

New York Mets third baseman David Wright backhands a ground ball during a baseball game against the Phillies on Tuesday, June 13, 2006, in Philadelphia. (AP Images)

today. I don't know of any Dick Williams or Billy Martin personalities managing today, and sometimes you need a guy like that.

I'm beginning to think Wright might be better off if he went someplace where he didn't have such a mental burden placed on him. For a lot of 2009, he was the only player on the field that was a *bone fide* major league starter, let alone a star. That team was dragging him down. He had 12 errors at the All-Star break. He's a better third baseman than that. It shows a lack of focus caused by having a load of pressure heaped on him. He thinks he has to do everything every game. I'd love to see what he'd do on a team where he could just play his game and let the other guys play theirs, instead of being the go-to guy for every reporter in New York every time the Mets spit the bit.

David tries not to give the writers any more ammunition than necessary. Some of the players say he speaks fluent *Bull Durham*, from all the clichés in that movie. He talks to everybody but never says anything to get anybody in trouble. No celebrations of hitting home runs with your finger in the air. That's just giving teams more reasons to want to beat your brains out. Hey, you're the Mets. There are already a lot of reasons to hate you. Why give them more?

For 2009, the Mets bought what everybody said they needed— a bullpen. I'm not sure they didn't have an edge on Philadelphia going into the start of the new season. Given how hard it is to repeat, a lot of smart baseball people picked the Mets over the Phillies before the season started.

Both teams started slowly again, and into June it looked like the Mets might put it together. Then the wheels fell off. And the fenders. And the headlights. Finally the driveshaft hit the pavement and the engine melted, as the Mets sustained more injuries than anybody can ever remember a team having. The Phillies got stronger as the year went on, just like in 2008. The 2009 team had a lot going for it.

Raul Ibanez did a good imitation of Carl Yastrzemski in 1967 until he went down with an injury. Maybe because he was in a new league and the pitchers didn't know him, he carried the team early. They needed somebody because again they were a .500 team until the weather warmed up. If Raul hadn't provided them some pop, they might have buried themselves early.

There was some concern that Utley's knee, which he finally got to rest in the off-season, would halt him a bit in 2009. I never thought it would. If you know anything about him at all, you knew he would recover from that injury way faster than forecast, because nobody works harder than Utley. He had another great year. I'm not alone in thinking he's the best second baseman in baseball.

Jimmy Rollins has had a down year as far as his batting average, but his doubles and home runs are up and he still fuels the Phillies' offense. I think he's been trying to do too much. Every now and then, Jimmy starts to think like a home-run hitter. When he's going good, he hits home-runs just because he's put a good swing on the ball, not because he's trying to hit them.

Ryan Howard is having another Ryan Howard year. Because he has a big body, some people thought he would not last, but he's established a high level of productivity and consistency. Mike Francesa, on New York City's WFAN-AM sports talk radio, called him the Willie McCovey of his generation. High praise, and right on.

Jamie Moyer started out the 2008 season with the same high expectations he and the fans always have for him. Now some people are saying he's finished. I don't think so. There isn't much a 45-year-old pitcher has that a 46-year-old doesn't, except maybe some kinder treatment from the umpires.

There have been a lot of games when he just couldn't get the ball where he wanted it, or he got it there and he didn't get the call. In order to get the strike call on the low outside corner, not to mention a few or several inches off it, you have to show the umpire that you can hit that spot consistently. If you don't, you won't get it when you *do* hit it. That forces Jamie to pitch toward the middle of the plate where the bat is. He's going to get hit.

But when he was taken out of the rotation, he was leading the team in wins! You might say he's had a bad year, but he's still going to get his wins and help the team.

Ryan Madson has had another good year, and that's important and rare in a setup guy. Between the starters and closer, you have five or six guys who are as important to winning as anybody but who are very difficult to get going well all at the same time. Look at any team that makes the playoffs, and those middle inning guys will have had good years.

Why do teams have trouble repeating? Because those same middle relievers may not be any good at all the next year. Happens all the time.

The Phillies middle inning guys have continued to be good. Chad Durbin, for instance. Madson did struggle a little when Lidge went on the disabled list. Ryan went into the closer's role and didn't know exactly what to expect. It's different pitching the ninth than it is the eighth. The experience helped him, and he learned something that will help him in the future.

As for Lidge, I think he would have been a lot better this year if he had just blown one save last year. He was a perfect 41 for 41. It's hard to improve upon perfection. There were high expectations on Lidge coming into 2009, and I'm sure his expectations were even higher.

He still has good stuff. It's just a matter of his believing in it. When you get into a down period as a closer, it seems like everything you throw is being hit. And with a closer, when you fail, everybody sees it and feels it. A hitter can hit .225 with no power for three months, and it will take time for it to sink in that he's not doing well. The closer has no place to hide.

That perfect record worked against him. He was like a young heavyweight boxing champion who gets knocked down for the first time. He thinks, "My God! What's going on? How could this happen?" Well, nothing's going on. It's just life. Nobody is perfect. Not for very long.

Brad thought he had to go out there and repeat perfection. I've said it all year long that he's gone to his put-away slider way too early on the count. You cannot strike out a guy on the first pitch. Let a hitter see your best pitch too often or too early, and it will get hit. Hitting is hard. When you start giving the hitters too much credit and feel like you have to throw your best pitch all the time, you make life way more difficult for yourself than it has to be.

You get ahead on the count with strikes. You get outs with balls. Watch when you see 3–2 counts in the ninth inning of close games. Notice how often a batter strikes out on ball four. The courage of a closer is not to throw your best pitch over the plate 3–2. It's to throw a pitch in the dirt, trusting the batter will swing. In those late-inning situations, most hitters are not thinking walk. They are thinking about getting their names in the paper and getting on the highlight video that night.

The Yankees and Red Sox played a 15-inning game in August that A-Rod won with a walk-off homer. From the ninth inning on, except for a Jeter at-bat and very few others, it was a Home Run Derby. Everybody was swinging to end it. That's why it took so long. If you ran video of every out recorded in the major leagues for a season, you will see way more outs made on balls than on strikes.

Cole Hamels has struggled, too, and nobody expected him to. I thought he was ready to be an ace for years to come. I still think he will be. The stats show that he has been throwing his fastball a little more and his change a little less, and that might be part of it, since he has a great change. But I think it is just that he was one of the biggest focuses for fans after winning the Series. You get all tied up with the crap that goes along with being a hero, and all of a sudden pitching is on the back burner.

I'm not saying it's his fault. He's a young guy, and when you get all that attention all of a sudden, it's hard to handle. That was true of the entire team, especially early in the season. They struggled at home because there were so many demands on their time. They couldn't wait to get on the road. As the season progressed, last year's championship faded into, "Well, that was last year," for both players and fans. Everybody then gets more focused on what you need to do this year.

Sometimes roles change from year to year even if players don't. When the Phillies kept Matt Stairs, it took away a lot of Greg Dobbs' pinch-hitting at-bats. Most closers are right-handed, and if they have good fastballs, Matt Stairs is the guy you want. At 40, he can still turn around anybody's fastball. So Greg has been hitting in different situations. Both are very valuable off the bench.

Don't take the stats of a bench player as any judge of his real value. When a hitter gets only a couple hundred at-bats a year, there can be wild statistical fluctuations from year to year. A role player has it to realize he's not Pete Rose if he hits .320 one year, and he isn't Willie Miranda if he hits .195 the next.

Players can get typecast. When the Phillies got Jayson Werth, most people saw him as a platoon or fourth outfielder. Turns out they got a power-hitting regular. Every contending team has stars that have to perform if the team is going anywhere. But what usually makes for success is not the stars having great years. They have them all the time. That's why they are stars. What makes teams big winners is when guys like Jayson do way more than they were expected to do. It makes a huge difference to write another 30-homer guy into your lineup that you didn't expect to have.

Keeping a team healthy from one year to the next is critical and often beyond anyone's control. As many pennants are lost through injuries as are won by great performances, maybe more. The Phillies have stayed pretty healthy, although Brett Myers went down with a torn labrum in his hip. I never heard of a torn labrum in a hip until the last couple of years, and now it seems like it is the "in" injury.

It makes me wonder. Why was everybody's labrum always fine until last year? I guess they didn't know what to call that kind of injury. Maybe it was just called "my butt hurts."

I was not surprised that Brett came back to help the team out of the bullpen during the playoffs. I think he is better in relief than he is as a starter anyway.

Just like you need more than your stars to perform to win anything, you need more than your ace to pitch well, too. Joe Blanton just goes out and does his thing every game. When the aces are going well, you hardly notice him. But this year, when Hamels and Moyer were struggling, he was the best starter the Phillies had. He doesn't get a lot of run support. He doesn't get many decisions because he doesn't go deep into a lot of games. He just continues to help as he has since the moment he came to the team.

I don't know where the Phillies would have been in 2009 without J.A. Happ, who compiled historically good stats for a Phillies rookie pitcher. If he's not the National League Rookie Pitcher of the Year, I don't know who is. Brad Lidge said Happ doesn't pitch like a rookie, and that's exactly right. He pitched a four-hit shutout against Colorado in August. He threw 127 pitches, and I guarantee 110 of them were fastballs no more than 89–92 mph.

Although he was a rookie in 2009, Phillies starter J.A. Happ sure didn't pitch like one. (AP Images)

Happ hides the ball well and locates well. In time, he will have to improve his secondary pitches, but right now it ain't broke, so don't fix it.

It also helps a team to go out and get two Cy Young Award winners. Cliff Lee and Pedro Martinez are at way different places in their careers, but both made huge impacts in the season and play-offs, obviously.

Even though the team didn't have that many player changes from 2008 to 2009, it has been a different year. Defending a championship is, like they always say, much harder than winning one. One thing hasn't changed, however, and that is Charlie Manuel. Well, one thing has changed around him—he gets more respect. And he should. I can't remember the last time somebody mentioned his accent. Rings will do that for you.

Chapter Five

Outside the Lines

I got married when I was 22, and I was way too immature to make a success of it. I don't think there are too many men alive who are ready to get married that young. There are probably some, but when I look back on it, I just was not one of them. Part of it was, "Hey, I'm grown up. I'm a big leaguer, right?" But I was not very grown up, as it turned out. We were married five years. We had no children. Eventually, we just didn't get along. Let's just call that first one a learning experience.

If you are not getting along with your wife, the separation necessary to be a ballplayer does not help one bit. It makes it worse.

My second marriage began right after the World Series in 1993. I was lucky in a way. My first child was born toward the end of my playing career, my second in 1995, when about all I had left was to get released a couple of times. Most of my parenting came after I had retired as a player. It is tough to be a dad while you are playing.

Not all that many players have their families living in the cities where they play, and if they do, they might move back somewhere in the off-season. Their family lives are divided by having two places to live, and there's a lot of moving between them.

Other guys don't have their families with them at all, even during home games. They live in hotels the whole season rather than buy a house or a condo because they know they are in a profession where you can suddenly wake up one day and find yourself working in another city.

Throw in the increasing number of players coming from outside the states, and you have a very high percentage of baseball players who just cannot be there for their families.

Yes, it is ironic that kids look up to us and maybe wish their dads could be ballplayers. If you ask the children of ballplayers, I bet a lot of them wish their dads would be mechanics or math teachers anything else as long as they were home.

Much of the responsibility for parenting falls on the wives of players, and it is difficult for them. Then when dad comes home, it's party time; let's have fun. He gets off the hook, or else he is forever fathering from behind. Really, it's not that much different from any profession where the husband travels a lot or works long hours. Life is life.

In fact, in some ways it's tougher for me now. I'm gone quite a bit, just about every night during the season when the Phillies play, or I'm driving back and forth from my home in south Jersey to the MLB-TV studios in Secaucus, across the river from Manhattan. It all comes down to the wife. If she can deal with it, then you have a good one.

Regardless of your family life, money is always a factor in a player's life, probably more than it is in most professions—because there is so much of it, and it is so closely linked to performance. Getting the big contract is just as often a stressful distraction to a player as it is security. Having your successes and failures in the paper every day, being compared to to every other guy who has your same job, will do that to you. I don't think there are any dentists or carpenters who have to go through anything like that, day in and day out.

In 1989, I finished in the top 10 in both the Cy Young and MVP voting. I led the league in appearances and was second in saves. For 1990, I signed a contract for more than a million dollars. It was my first big paycheck.

Of course, in my mind I was already rolling in dough when I got an $18,000 bonus coming out of high school. I bought an American Motors Concord, a little car with a big V-8 engine and thought I was living high. My first year in the majors, I went a little higher shelf for my wheels and got an IROC Camaro, which had a little more giddy up than the usual street model. It wasn't like I got a Porsche or Lamborghini or something. I was never going to spend huge sums of money on a car. I guess that was the way I was raised. I view a vehicle more as a tool than a status symbol. I've driven a pickup truck for the last 25 years or so. (No, not the same one.)

There are some ways to save money. For instance, Cole Hamels got the new version of the Camaro for being the MVP of the 2008 World Series.

Some players go out and buy big cars or expensive watches and jewelry right away. I played with a guy years ago that made $60,000 and he showed up at spring training in a $60,000 car! My goodness, I thought. I guess he figured he'd be getting a raise before too long. As it turned out, he did not. I told him, "I hope you like that car, because you're going to be sleeping in it, the way you're hitting."

Aside from the car, the first thing I did when I got to the big leagues was have a mole taken off my face, and I had my front teeth shortened. That was what was important to me. Eventually, I got a ranch down in Texas. That's all I ever wanted.

That big paycheck does have some other kinds of consequences. One thing you discover is that when a ballplayer makes a bad decision in marriage, and a lot of us do, he is going to write a big check. A *big* check. This experience gave me some of the wisdom I only thought I had when I got married the first time.

Big money can be very confusing in many ways. Once I started getting my paychecks based on that big contract, I asked that they be sent to my agent. I didn't want to be distracted by any of that stuff. One time they made a mistake and sent it to me. I looked at it. Ballplayers get paid every two weeks. By that point in the season, I had paid $95,000 in taxes! I could not wrap my mind around that.

I came from a very lower-middle-class family. My father was making maybe $50,000 a year then, and I paid way more than that just in taxes. How are you supposed to make sense of that? Who you are is important, not what you make. I just wanted to be me. Whatever money I made, that was just a blessing. I never felt that making a lot of money made anybody important or special.

It is not unusual for a player who has just signed a monster contract to struggle. They don't believe they are worth the money, and they try to do more than they can to justify their salary. That won't work.

I've played with some men who never believed they were worth the money they were being paid. Mark Davis was one of them. He won the Cy Young Award and led the league in saves in 1989. He went to Kansas City as a free agent, getting a contract way bigger than mine. That was his last good year.

Mark was one of the nicest people you'd ever want to meet, and I think he just tried too hard to justify his contract. He won the Cy Young Award. What more could he do? The answer was that he didn't have to do anything other than what he had been doing, but the money messed with his head. He was never the same pitcher again.

Everybody around the game is aware that salaries get jacked up way more because of arbitration than free agency. People who wouldn't know a save from a hook slide decide whether the players' or the owners' salary figures will prevail. I never went there.

Ty Cobb was always thinking ahead of the pitchers back in his day, and he was thinking ahead of the owners after he retired. Those congressional hearings about steroids weren't the first time politicians investigated baseball. There were hearings in 1953 about whether baseball was a monopoly. Current Supreme Court Justice John Paul Stevens was one of the legal councils for the committee. The reserve clause, which bonded players to their teams indefinitely, was a major concern. Most players defended the reserve clause, not wanting to rock the boat since the owners had demonstrated their willingness many times to throw overboard anyone who did.

Cobb, long-retired and rich more from investments than playing salary because he got in on the ground floor of a couple of new companies called Chevrolet and Coca-Cola, suggested the radical idea that players and owners might go to arbitration after a player's fifth year. It was almost exactly what the player's association got decades later.

I never wanted to go to arbitration. I always believed that if you pay me what's fair, I'd sign. Of course, I am aware that arbitration and free agency encourages ownership toward fairness more than a little bit. Still, I always thought the arbitration process looked wrong to the fans. And it felt wrong to me. I never wanted to fight over money in a courtroom.

I was a free agent with the Phillies in 1991 and I just signed with them again. I never tested the market. I never negotiated with another team. I made it clear to them that all I wanted was what was fair, and they were more than fair. I got a big bump in salary to more than $3 million a year, the most I ever made.

Today you hear more about players being more motivated in their "walk year," after which they can become free agents. The Yankees A.J. Burnett was viewed with some skepticism when he signed because his two best years were both years when he would be a free agent. The implication is that a player isn't as hungry and might not give his best effort until it comes time for a new payday.

I'd like to think that's not true, because if it is, I think it is kind of disgusting. I was always hungry because in my mind I was always playing to earn the money they were already paying me. I never pitched to earn money in the future.

That was why, when I messed up my knee trying to cover first base in 1990, I didn't have surgery. I tore my posterior cruciate ligament. If I had surgery, I would have been out a minimum of 18 months. I didn't think it was fair for me to sit out that long when I was being paid all that money.

I was told I could rebuild the knee if I went into the weight room and blasted my quads. I was out 30 days and mostly lived in the weight room. It was the only time I was ever on the disabled list, and I was miserable.

I gave everything I had every time I went out on the mound. That's just the way I was. In the long run, some people may think that wasn't the smartest thing to do. If I had stayed out a year and had surgery, my knee might have been stronger. I might have lasted longer. Who knows? That just wasn't me.

After their Carl Pavano experience, it's a little strange that the Yankees signed Burnett if they thought he was not sufficiently motivated to pitch. Carl basically sat out his entire four-year contract with one injury and complaint after another until it was about ready to run out. Then toward the end of the season, he was suddenly in the rotation! He pitched just enough to get another contract, this time with the Indians. The Yankees fans hated him. You hate to say that anyone is not hurt, but there are some guys who will play through anything, and there are other guys who will play through nothing.

I never got sent down once I was up, except toward the end of my career, when I was trying to rehab. There are guys getting sent down today that I don't understand. They have nothing more to prove. David Price was sent down. That guy was a huge reason the Rays got to the Series. Even if they don't think he is ready to start, couldn't he help them out of the bullpen until he was?

The Orioles sent down catcher Matt Wieters. He hit like Babe Ruth in the minors last year. So now they want him to "prove himself" in Triple A? The Orioles opening-day catcher was Gregg Zaun. Nothing against Gregg, but Baltimore is not going to build their future around him.

Now if a kid is on the bubble, fighting for the last spot on the bench or the bullpen, that is different. Or if you have a star at the kid's position who is not going to get moved out of there. You don't want a future star to languish on a big-league bench when he could be developing sooner by playing every day in the minors. I understand that.

But Price and Wieters were not sent down for those reasons. It was money, pure and simple. If they start the year in the minors, their teams can delay their arbitration and free agency a whole year. The Red Sox did that with Roger Clemens when he was a rookie.

I have a real problem with a club doing this for one reason: they are not putting their best ball club on the field because they are not putting their 25 best players on the roster. They are making roster decisions not for performance reasons but for financial reasons. They are cheating the fans out of seeing the best team they could field, and they are cheating the players out of part of their careers.

What kind of relationship are you building with these kids, around whom you supposedly want to build your future? They are obviously going to be frustrated, no matter what they tell the media. And when they do come to arbitration or free agency, how are they going to feel about being cheated out of that year? Are they going to want to sign with that team? It all seems penny wise and pound foolish to me.

Whether a guy stays up or is sent down, and who wins in arbitration is determined more and more by statistics. Stats have always been important in baseball. There just have never been so many of them—with more every year.

The only stat I ever cared about was if I walked on the field with the lead that we had it when I walked off. It was all about team wins and losses for me. But I tell you, it's hard for a manager when the players have it in their contracts to be paid according to individual stats. How does a manager tell a pitcher who is going to make an extra $50,000 if he gets 30 saves again this year that he is going to to be a setup guy?

The question is whether or not you are doing your job. If Ryan Howard hits .330 but drives in only 50 runs, what good is that? I couldn't care less about his batting average. I care about how many guys he chases across the plate. As long as you know your job description and perform it, you will get paid.

How do you work for wins when you get paid on your stats? It all depends on the player. If you go out there and your only objective is to win, and you do, you'll get paid. If you are worried about being the highest paid this or that, you are worried about the wrong thing. I didn't play for money; I played for fun. If I were only playing for money, I would have kept playing. I believe that even today I could take six weeks, get my body in shape, come back, and make a very nice living just getting left-handers out. But I wanted to be able to get *everybody* out! It all comes down to what is important to the player: how much money is in his bank account, or the pride that comes along with being successful, a winner. I cared more about the pride than I did about the paycheck. Pride or paycheck?

All these new stats also drown the fan. They are overused by a lot of writers and broadcasters. I don't think fans are all that interested in them. If I were watching a game, I'd want to hear more about why this happened or what *should* have happened. I want to tell fans what teams are trying to do and whether they are doing it.

Just giving stats is a lazy way to work. You get the stat sheet in front of you. You can say so-and-so is four for his last 28 with runners in scoring position, or you can tell how he's going to be pitched and what he is trying to do during that at-bat. Hitting averages are almost random until you get a few hundred at-bats. That a guy is hitting .400 in his last 10 games really tells you nothing about how he's going to do today, or even how he has been doing recently. Hitting .400 is 18-for-45. He might have five seeing-eye bleeders and be fighting off a slump, or he might have had five two-iron shots caught at the warning track and be on fire. Guys ought to report what they see, not just give numbers. Of course, maybe some guys are not too sure what they are seeing.

Every big leaguer is not fighting just the tough pitchers and hitters. The money does a number on your head. Family life is tough. And there are other distractions. Sometimes the distractions become something way worse.

I played with Steve Howe. He was definitely troubled. That's not news. We got him in '87 after I don't know how many rehabs and suspensions. Right after the season finished, we had a mini camp when we came in for a week just to throw. Steve came the first day, then disappeared. It would be four years before he got back into a big-league uniform.

You could just look at him and see the face of addiction. It just had a hold on him. You can never tell who is going to get hooked. Some people are a total train wreck; others are very gifted and keep coming back, like Steve. When you get suspended seven times and they still let you come back because somebody wants you on their team, that's talent. It is also somebody who at bottom is a decent guy. Even a world-class fastball won't keep a bad apple employed forever.

With Steve, a lot of things came together that caused problems. It wasn't just a lot of different drugs, but the stuff that comes with the drugs: fast cars, motorcycles, guns. There's no telling what a healthy Howe might have done. But with Steve, it had a hold on him, and it was always hard for me to believe that he was ever going to get over it.

Darrell Porter was another troubled guy. His last two years in the majors were my first two. It had been a few years since he confessed his drug use after a conference with Don Newcombe. The former Dodgers great, whose own career had been cut short by alcoholism, was an addiction counselor employed by Major League Baseball. Darrell went into rehab and changed his life completely. By the time he played with me, he was an occasional catcher but a very regular friend. He was a great communicator with the young players and might have made a great manager. If you ever wanted to talk about the game, or if you needed any advice or support on anything, Darrell was one of the first people I'd go to. You don't find many like him, inside baseball or outside either. I loved that guy. Yet after years of being straight, his heart stopped and they found toxic levels of cocaine in his system.

Alcohol has been a factor in baseball as long as there has been baseball. A brewery was among the sponsors of the Cincinnati Red Stockings, the first professional team, back in 1869. Fans like a beer at the park as much as players like one after the game. I drank my share of beer, and in Philadelphia we stayed in the clubhouse all hours of the night, drinking beer and talking baseball. Yet alcohol abuse was never a factor on the teams I was on. You never had to look the other way because you thought, "Oh, oh, that guy's out of control."

It all comes down to responsibility. You have to be able to handle what you are doing. As for drugs, I just never understood that. I found out I could get in more than enough trouble without doing things that were illegal.

There is a lot more counseling on teams than there used to be, and I think players are more aware of the dangers now. The guys who are going to drink and drug themselves out of the game are usually going to do it before they reach the majors. I played with one guy in the minors, that would have shocked me if he made it to 21. You can tell a guy that if this is what he wants to do for a living, he can't be high or hammered all the time. Not everybody is going to listen.

It's like when you are in college. People will flunk out of college as freshman because they drink too much. Seniors hardly ever do. If you are going to succeed, you learn how to handle it.

Alcohol abuse can become a problem again after a player retires. It can arise because of too much time on your hands, maybe a few blows to the ego because nobody is chasing you for your autograph or comping you into everything. It's a radical change of lifestyle, and you have to learn how to be you all over again with the same temptations.

There has been no greater challenge to personal responsibility in the baseball business than steroids. One of the worst things about the "steroid era" is that the subject is like kudzu; it just takes over everything. It has colored just about everything in baseball for some time now and shows no sign of going away, even with testing and a greater awareness of the dangers.

I first heard of steroids in the late 1980s. I played against Jose Canseco in rookie ball when he looked like he weighed about 185 pounds. A couple of years later, he's like 250. Everybody wondered what was going on. You just don't put on that kind of muscle mass. We all knew it was something, but it was not talked about.

Baseball players, not to mention front-office types, had never seen anything like that before. Each year there were more guys like him. What always scared me away from them was what I heard it did to your sex life. I mean, I would think that would discourage everybody, but I guess I'm wrong.

Performance enhancing? Okay. But life shortening? It might enhance your performance but it shortens your life. What kind of trade is that? In the grand scheme of things, baseball is not that much of it. I've been retired for 12 years as of 2009, and I only played 11 seasons. Are those 10, 12, even 20 years of your life in exchange for a very few professional seasons worth all that? So you make a ton of money. Any decent player is going to make a ton. Does it really matter if you make two or three tons if you die when you are 50? You made a fortune and got yourself so messed up you died young or couldn't enjoy it.

There are a lot of aspects of steroid use that make me angry, besides the just plain cheating of it. Now with any great performance, people are going to wonder if the player was juiced. It has never been proven that Roger Clemens took steroids. People suspect him because he maintained such a high level of performance for so long.

Jose Canseco watches his own home run in the third inning against the Toronto Blue Jays on Saturday, October 7, 1989, in Toronto. (AP Images)

Some people have even speculated that Nolan Ryan was an early adapter to steroids for the same reason. And Ryan was Clemens' idol. What people don't realize is that we are talking about two examples of players who worked out to a level that "normal" people can't even conceive of. Ryan did an hour on the bike *after* he pitched a complete game. He had a bike program Lance Armstrong would have trouble maintaining. So when a player has a super season, don't automatically say, "He had to be on something."

What if a player led the league by hitting 20 more homers than the guy who finished second? He had to have been juiced, right? Either that or he was Mickey Mantle in 1956 when he hit 52. Vic Wertz was second with 32.

Suppose there was a guy who was known to have the biggest muscles in the league. Suppose, after hitting more than 20 homers only once in his first five years, he suddenly went for 40-plus three years in a row. Then suppose that after one more good year, he only got into double digits once again in his whole career. The guy obviously went on steroids, then off. Or he was Ted Kluszewski, whose three big power years were 1953–55. He then suffered a severe back injury, which robbed him of his power. MLB television has shown the film of the 1959 World Series when Ted hit three homers. If you ever want to see a guy hit with no hip rotation, no back flexibility, it was Big Klu at the end of his career.

If a hitter won the batting title at age 38 with his highest batting average in 16 years, he'd have to be on something, right? Either that or he was Ted Williams, who hit .388 in 1957.

And what about the guy who led the league in homers and had almost three times as many as the next guy! That was Babe Ruth in 1919, when he had 29 and the next highest total was 10. We all know that Babe was powered by hot dogs and beer.

It is hard not to be cynical, and I think that probably a lot of the stats we saw in the last decade or so are suspect. But not every great performance is.

What bothers me most about this stuff is the way that the stories are reported. First, let's remember that most writers and broadcasters weren't exactly Woodward and Bernstein when it came to investigating steroid use. Some writers don't want to cast Hall of Fame votes for players they think were on steroids—fine. I don't think any writers or broadcasters should go into their respective wings of the Hall of Fame if they spent most of the steroid era oohing and ahhing over all the homers instead of being just a bit more curious.

Even today the media does a disservice by going on and on about A-Rod, Manny, Sosa, Clemens, Bonds, McGwire, and other stars who are under suspicion or have been confirmed as users. The problem is that young athletes only hear about the great players who took steroids or might have.

The truth is that most of the users were not stars. Look at the Mitchell Report. Most of the names there do not even rise to the level of marginal. Manny made big news when he got a 50-game suspension for testing positive. He is not the only one who has received this penalty. Remember who the other players were? That's my point.

Ryan Franklin got popped. Who the hell is he? He got caught in 2005 when he was 8–15 with an earned run average over 5.00. If he was enhancing to achieve that performance, what would it have been if he were straight! This year he's an All-Star closer and presumably clean.

What kids have to have driven home to them is that although steroids *may* be performance enhancing; they are not in any way talent-bestowing. They might help you hit a fly ball farther, but they are not going to help you hit that 90-mph slider in the first place. If you are a pitcher, it might help you recover more quickly, but it won't help you hit a corner. Part of the reason for so many big flies in the 1990s was that there were more pitchers able to throw 90 but not more who were able to throw 90 with *good location*. More fast pitches thrown in hitters' happy zones just make for more homers, not more successful pitchers.

You can take all the drugs you want. If you don't have the ability, you aren't playing this game. The sick thing about some players is that they were going into the Hall of Fame anyway, way before they might have started using, and now, who knows? As usual, it will depend a lot on performance, and for some on how well a player was liked.

Barry Bonds was a great player, which is no news flash. Personally, I did not like him, which is also not exactly an unusual opinion. I believe that you can be the best at what you do and still be personable and good to people. He was just hard to like. I know if I were the best at what I did, I'd be the happiest guy in the world, the most jovial guy on the planet. No one loves Barry more than Barry. That's who he is.

Barry spiked our second baseman in a game that had gotten out of hand in Pittsburgh. They called for me to pitch to Barry, and I knew why I was coming in. I did what was necessary, and Bonds started to the mound. I told him, like I told every hitter who took a step toward me, "You can come out here. I might win or you might win, but understand that if you do, I promise you I will hit you every time you come to bat." He went to first.

Bonds was a good hitter long before steroids. Did he get bigger? Yes, he did. Steroids are illegal because of the terrible things they can do to your body. Players should not take them, period. I think the impact of steroids on baseball as it is played on the field is way overblown. It was only one of many factors. Smaller parks. The seams on the balls they use now make them feel more like billiard balls than baseballs. It is pretty darn hard to get a wrinkle on a pitch when you can't grab a seam. But far and away the biggest factor is this—taking the inside of the plate away from pitchers put a lot more pitches over the fence than any chemicals.

You can't have kids believing if they take steroids they will become like Alex Rodriguez or Barry Bonds. That is way worse than when Spike Lee did those commercials about Nike Air Jordans and said, "It's the shoes, man. It's the shoes." It isn't the shoes, and it isn't the steroids. It's the natural ability and the willingness to work at it.

If I'm talking to any young kid or his parents, the first thing I'm going to tell them is, "Do not make this kid play just one sport." I think the biggest crime right now in youth sports is that parents are taking kids—not even teenagers, but kids who are eight or nine—and having them play baseball year-round. They don't have them play anything else. They are just making kids hate baseball. It will burn out their interest. It's become a job.

You have to be able to hold a kid's interest. Keep it fun. Not only does this burn out the kid, it doesn't make him a better athlete. An athlete is someone who can play sports, period, not just do one thing.

High school is going to tell youngsters which sport they are going to play. Go with your strength then. I played a lot of sports all through high school, but I knew I was too light to keep playing football and too slow for basketball. There isn't much of a market for real wrestlers, and I had an exceptionally strong arm. It didn't take a genius to figure out which way for me to go.

Once there is the talent and the desire, you have to change gears. It can't just be fun anymore. Not once you decide you want to be a professional, or even a scholarship athlete in college. You become like any other professional. It becomes a job. Sure it has to be fun, in a way. But it won't always be fun. No profession ever is. You have to have the god-given ability and the tenacity to keep working at it, improving, and adjusting to new challenges all the time.

I grew up with two brothers. My older brother was my hero. I wanted to do everything like he did, but I wanted to do it even better. There is a national competition called Pass, Punt and Kick that was started in 1961. It is divided into different age groups. When I was eight, I won the Portland, Oregon, regional competition for nine-year-olds. My parents couldn't afford to send me to the nationals, but I got a huge trophy. My older brother was pissed because I had a big trophy and he didn't.

I remember my father saying to him, "How many times have I seen you out in the yard by yourself, kicking and throwing your football?" I didn't need anybody in order to practice. When I was a kid, if there was a baseball game on, I'd watch for two or three innings, then I had to go out and *play* baseball. It was the same with all sports. I liked to watch, but I could only watch for a little while. I had to go out and *do* it.

There is no reason for a kid with talent to worry about getting known. Scouting is no secret society. If there is a kid who has something special, everybody is going to know. I do believe that fans never see some of the best arms, because they get burned out in high school or college, but that isn't necessarily because they throw too much. If a high school pitcher hurts his arm, I believe it is much more likely to be from bad mechanics or breaking pitches. I don't believe you get burned-out just by throwing. In high school, I started twice a week: Tuesday and Friday.

I think you have to wait on breaking pitches, but that won't hurt a young player's ability to get scouted. If he throws hard, all the other things can be developed later. If your arm is good enough to get you signed, it is good enough to dominate in high school just with fastballs. Besides, a lot of guys with hard-throwing fast-balls have natural movement anyway. Some have a natural sinker.

I don't even think kids should mess with cutters or sliders, or moving pitches that don't require a lot of rotation of the elbow or shoulder. The problem is, every kid, once he sees a little break, wants to see more. They start trying to get a little more break, and that leads to trouble when the arm bones and tissues are not fully developed.

There are ways to teach around this a little. My 13-year-old wants to throw a breaking ball. I taught him to hold the ball like a football and release it like a football. It breaks a little bit and gives the kid what he wants to see. But it won't hurt his arm. Yes, it's a little like Carlton's or Guidry's slider, but my son's not going to throw 50 of them at 90 mph. For him, it's an off-speed pitch.

If you find your son has enough arm speed to get somebody's attention in high school, or if you are a coach of a kid like that, my biggest advice would be to get him mechanically sound and teach him to locate his fastball. That is the biggest hurdle when you go to college or the minor leagues. You have many kids with good arms, but they can't throw strike one. Learn to locate your fastball, and everything else will follow. I wish I had been able to follow that advice better than I did.

Even in the major leagues, locating the fastball is key. The pitching in the 2009 All-Star Game was awesome. The one thing all those pitchers have in common is that they can locate their fast-balls. They put it right where they want it most of the time. They may have all different kinds of different secondary pitches. There were a lot of pitchers sitting at home watching that game who have just as much stuff or more, but they can't locate the fastball. People can argue about it, but for me it is settled. The fastball is the best pitch in baseball. It has been for more than a hundred years, and it will be for the next hundred.

Dominating high school pitchers are bigger local celebrities today than they were back in my day, maybe because the bonuses to high draft choices are so off the charts now. The first time I was asked to give an autograph was when I was still in high school. We won the state championship in Portland, and I got asked. Surprised the hell out of me. Of course, I got asked a lot once I turned pro, even in rookie ball.

I remember one of the few times I ever asked anybody for an autograph was in the visitors' dugout at Fenway Park. They were having an Old Timers Day, and Joe DiMaggio was in our dugout. I was in uniform. I took a ball over and said, "Mr. DiMaggio, could you sign this?" He looked me right in the eye and said no. I never looked at DiMaggio the same after that.

If you tell someone no, that person is someone who has soured on you *for life*. You are literally talking about two seconds of your life, longer if you are Jarrod Saltalamacchia. You don't have that much time for someone who admires what you do?

I never said no to autographs. I consider it an honor to be asked. As any autograph hound knows, there is zero correlation between a player's ability on the field and his willingness to sign. It has nothing to do with how good a player he is and everything to do with how good a person he is. I have no use for players who turn down kids.

I've signed during dinner. I understand that this is one time that it just comes down to manners. My father, if nothing else, made sure we had manners. You were going to have manners or you were going to get smacked, that's all there was to it. I understand not wanting to sign during dinner because that's a private time even if it is a public place. But I always signed after I was finished.

This kind of attention should not be a big thing, or something that surprises players. Certainly if you are a superstar and get recognized all over the country and not just in your team's hometown, it should not come as a shock. Anybody who gets involved in the world of professional athletics should know what comes with the territory.

Even I have some limits. I've gotten stacks of 50 baseball cards in the mail, obviously from card dealers. I'll sign two and send the rest back.

I've signed at card shows for fees. The people who go to those shows are hardcore collectors and dealers, and I understand that there is a business aspect to this kind of thing. I always tell the promoter that if a child comes up and doesn't have a ticket, I'm still signing. A little kid might not understand what is going on.

I had a box of baseball cards when I was a kid. There must have been 10,000 cards in there. I didn't mess with them a lot and naturally, I have no idea what happened to them. Like most pro athletes, I'm not a big collector of sports memorabilia.

Some guys are. I remember Curt Schilling sending clubhouse boys to opposing dugouts to get stuff signed. I did one thing like that my entire career. I really liked Deion Sanders as a football player and thought he could be a good baseball player, too. When we played the Braves, he had just come out with those "Neon Deion" Nikes. I walked up to him before batting practice one day and asked if he'd give me a pair.

He said he'd love to trade a pair for one of my red gloves. I felt pretty good about that, and the clubhouse boys made the exchange. I put them in my locker and after the game somebody had taken them from my locker. I guess they were a little too hot of an item at the time.

I think I was among the first to wear a colored glove regularly. I started in Chicago, when I was under contract to Wilson and they came out with a glove the exact same blue as the Cubbie blue. I thought that looked cool, so I started wearing them in 1989.

Red Sox pitcher Curt Schilling signed autographs for fans and collected them from other players. (AP Images)

Wilson made me the red gloves when I moved to Philadelphia. They had "Wild 99" stitched on them.

I also have a few jerseys, balls, and bats at home. I have the ball from when I broke the Phillies single-season save record. I don't have a lot of photographs or mementoes displayed at home. If you come to my house, you will see a couple of framed jerseys in the foyer. That's it. I don't need anything around to remind me that I played.

Chapter Six

The End of the Road

Whenever you hear a player over 35 years old say at the beginning of spring training, "I'm in the best shape of my life," that is never true. He thinks he's in better shape because he might never have worked harder to get in shape. He's worked harder, so he thinks he's in better shape. Trust me, he's not.

I agree with the stat people that most players peak around 27 or 28. Most players are free agents at least a couple of years after they peak. General managers pay top dollar for free agents over 30, then act surprised when they don't perform as well as they did when they were younger.

Some guys will more than make up for what they lose physically by taking advantage of what they have learned. They have made the adjustments necessary to compensate for the aging process, at least for a few years. I was not one of those players. I never changed my approach to pitching, and that is a regret I have.

I was still counting on being able to throw fastballs by people when my speed was not what it had once been. I was too hardheaded. Instead of learning different pitches, I just wanted to keep going at it the way I always had. When I couldn't do it anymore, I had to retire.

When I look back on it, there wasn't all that much I needed to learn. Yes, I had a knee injury that ultimately killed my career. But long before that, all I needed to figure out how to do was move the ball a few inches back in my hand, change speeds. Or move my fingers a little off-center on the seams so it would cut into a right-handed hitter. It doesn't seem like much now, and it might have prolonged my career several years. At the time, I just couldn't see it.

My partner on MLB television, Dan Plesac, was a very successful closer who ran into trouble in his late twenties, like I did. He completely reinvented himself and pitched a total of 18 years until he was 41. That wasn't me. I was a "here's my heat, try to hit it" guy, and when they did, that was it.

Guys who start pretty young, like I did around 21 or 22, have a hard time maintaining their performance into their thirties. Sometimes the better athletes, who got by on pure physicality, can't survive once they lose just a bit of their physical advantage. Other guys, who maybe didn't have as much physical ability at that young age, sometimes last longer because they don't depend on just being great athletes. They had to learn more about the game to make the big leagues, so they continue to learn.

A guy like Jamie Moyer has made a million adjustments. He's won twice as many games in his forties than he did in his twenties! He was striking out hitters in 2008 at a higher rate than many of his earlier years. The 2008 Phillies might not have gone anywhere without his 16 wins. A pitcher has to either throw above hitting speed or below it. He figured out that as he got older, he could still throw pitches below hitting speed and be effective.

What do I mean by hitting speed? A pitcher with a dominant fastball can overpower hitters. He throws above hitting speed. The ball will cross the plate before the bat does. But a pitcher can also miss bats by throwing *below* bat speed. The bat crosses the plate before the pitch arrives. Same result: a swing and a miss.

Now, when you throw right at bat speed, you have to locate every pitch, hit the corners, and outguess the hitter every time because every mistake is going to be hit somewhere and often very hard. You can make a mistake above bat speed because the hitter is going to be late, or below because the hitter is already committed and off his front foot. It's tough to make a mistake when the hitter's loaded and his timing is perfect.

There is a time of adjustment after a pitcher loses his good fastball and before he's learned to throw below hitting speed that is a very dangerous time in a career, even for the great ones. Robin Roberts, the best Phillies pitcher between Grover Cleveland Alexander and Steve Carleton, went 1–10 in 1961 after winning 10 or more in 12 consecutive years, including six years with 20 or more wins. He was sold to the Yankees, where he showed so little he was released before the end of spring training. The Orioles signed him for nothing, expecting the same.

Yet he turned in four more winning seasons, with victory totals of 10, 14, 13, and 10. Though he was no longer an ace, he had become a useful pitcher again. How? He made the adjustment from throwing above bat speed to below. While he once threw one of the best fastballs in baseball, he was the last player in the National League to know that he had lost it.

Here again Baltimore manager Paul Richards helped a pitcher make a vital adjustment. He was one of the few managers in major-league history who was a gifted teacher of pitching techniques. His specialty was teaching how to change speeds. He called his prime weapon "the slip pitch," and he tried to teach it to everybody on his pitching staff. He found a willing student in Roberts, one of the smartest guys who ever played the game. Robin slipped his way to 52 wins once he reached aged 35, giving him a career total of 286. Richards' changeup proved to be an engraved invitation to the Hall of Fame, addressed to Robin Roberts.

Mike Mussina announced his retirement at the end of the 2008 season with 270 career victories and is considered a borderline Hall of Famer. Hanging around a few more years, maybe winning 300 would have made him a more attractive candidate. And he retired after winning 20 games! The last pitcher to do that was Sandy Koufax, but he was only 30 and retired after winning 27 and the Cy Young Award because he was having circulation problems in his arm. His problems were not only career-threatening but life threatening. He didn't have much choice but to retire.

Winning 20 is a great way to go out. For a guy to win 20 and announce his retirement, to me that says he just doesn't have it in him anymore. The mental discipline just isn't there. It's not physical. He might have just woke up one morning after the season was over and said to himself, "You know, I just don't want to do what I have to do to get ready to do that again."

For years, Mussina's strikeout totals had been going down and his hit totals going up. That he got as far as 270 wins is a testament to his ability to make adjustments. Playing for a good team doesn't hurt, either. He knows better than anyone what kind of stuff he still has and whether or not it is likely to get people out in another year or two or three.

You can go out there and get by without doing all the preparation, all the hard work that goes along with it, and still have some success. But then he's cheating himself and the people he's playing with and the people who are paying him. Nobody else knows the price that Mussina might have paid for the success he had in 2008. He'll be 40 before the end of the 2009 season. I'm sure somebody would have paid him another $15 million to give it a try, but if you can't give everything you've got, walk away. You've got to admire that attitude.

Velocity is the most obvious thing that starts to go. Once you lose your fastball, you don't get it back. Arm speed is God's gift.

Yankees starter Mike Mussina retired after the 2008 season, just 30 victories shy of 300. (AP Images)

When you lose it, you either learn to pitch around it or you get lit up. I didn't pitch around it very well. I lost velocity, and I didn't have a bunch of other pitches to fall back on.

Gaylord Perry's strikeouts stayed pretty consistent until the age of 42. Then it dipped, but he was able to hang on a few more years, add to his win total, and get over the Hall of Fame threshold of 300 wins. Sure, he had a hundred different pitches, including the threat or the reality of the spitter, but what really kept him winning was the ability to throw a good fastball, even if it was only used five or six times a game.

He would frustrate hitters with endless dinky curves and sinkers low and away. Then he would zip one under a guy's chin every other inning or so. That kept everybody from diving across the plate. Once he couldn't gear up to throw hard even that often, he went back to his farm.

Some say a pitcher gains some velocity after Tommy John surgery, or the surgery that removes a rib from the side of their pitching arm, which allows for more arm movement and increases circulation. I'm not so sure about that. I believe that arm speed is arm speed. You either have it or you don't. A pitcher might be able to come back after surgery to where he was right before, and maybe even keep it longer, but that's it. He won't throw harder.

It's the exact same thing with hitting. Bat speed is key. When you lose bat speed, there are adjustments that must be made. Toward the end of his career, when Pete Rose was trying to beat Ty Cobb's record for most career hits, his bat was completely flat. He had zero bat speed. The only thing he could do was make the bat pass through the zone when the ball was there. The only way to do that without bat speed is to flatten out your swing and just slap at the ball. That's what Pete did—just put the ball in play. He never had a slugging average over .400 after the age of 38.

Aging power hitters need a different strategy. They survive slowing bat speed by yielding part of the plate. You can only guard so much of the strike zone. So you see guys foul off pitches they used to hammer and miss pitches they used to foul. The result is that they might still hit some homers but do so with lower batting averages. Reggie Jackson averaged almost 20 homers during his last five years after he turned 37, but he only managed a .227 batting average.

As a pitcher, you've got to see when a hitter is giving you part of the plate and when he is ahead or behind your stuff. This kind of recognition by pitchers today seems to be sorely lacking. You see hitters foul balls straight back. What do you always hear, from the dugout to the broadcast booth to the stands? "Oh God, he's on that one! He just missed it!" Wrong.

If he fouled it straight back, he's *not* on it. He's late. Think about it a minute. Every ball falls as it approaches the plate. A good fastball appears to rise because it falls less than normal. So a hitter that fouls a pitch straight back is hitting the bottom of the ball. He's expecting the ball to fall more than it has. He's *late*.

I've watched great hitters trick pitchers into throwing them breaking balls by fouling the fastball straight back. I've played with some hitters and that's all they did. Larry Parrish, when we were with the Rangers, couldn't wait to trick pitchers into throwing him a slider when he fouled a pitch straight back. Because he had a slider speed bat, he couldn't get around on great heat. He made his living for years by hitting sliders because pitchers believed he was "on" the fastball that he fouled straight back. They'd almost *always* follow that fastball he fouled back with a slider that he'd wait for and pound. He'd hit that slider nine miles. He hit more with his brain than his bat. Geez, if he was "on" the fastball, he would have *hit* the fastball! Some guys can't play once their bat slows down to slider speed. Parrish lived there and thrived. Adjustments.

A number of things can slow down bat and arm speed. It isn't always arm injuries or aging. In my case, it was knee injuries. I never had any arm problems until my last year in Kansas City. Even that was something I could have worked through. It was my right knee. I'd get to a certain point in my delivery, and my right leg would collapse. If I couldn't get everything on it, it was useless for me to pitch.

It was because of the decision I made after I tore up the knee in Chicago, strengthening it in the weight room instead of having surgery. I got back on the field sooner, but the knee was always a problem after that. It got to the point where I was going in every two years and getting chips taken out. Then I had my femur and kneecap shaved down because the knee would lock up. It got to the point where it wasn't worth it any more. My arm was okay, but my knee was shot and what was worse, my heart just wasn't in it. A player can survive a lot, but when the heart goes, he's done.

A lot of different things can influence how long a guy plays, or tries to. When I got traded out of Philadelphia about six weeks after the 1993 World Series, mentally that was probably it for me, but I didn't know it at the time. I hung around for a few more years, but it wasn't fun anymore on any level. They traded Babe Ruth, so they can trade anybody. Anyone who is traded needs to view it not so much that your old team didn't want you, but that your new team does. "Don't let a trade bother you," everybody says. It isn't that easy.

Soon after I got to Houston in 1994, I had a personality conflict with the manager, Terry Collins. I met with general manager Bob Watson. I said, "Bob, I'll do any job you want me to do, but I've earned the right to know what the job is." If they didn't have a job for me to do, fine. Release me. They did.

I didn't pitch all that well while I was there, I admit. But I'd walk in every day not knowing what my job was what was expected of me. If they didn't want me to close, that was fine with me. I'd do anything, but I wanted to know what my role would be. I think that's the least anybody on the roster can expect.

They released me just before the strike. Nobody likes to be released, but it could not have come at a better time. I was one of the few players who still got paid!

I signed with the Angels for 1995 and pitched about as badly for them as I did in Houston and got released in June. I just rested my knee and tried to get back into shape then signed with the Phillies again for 1996. I went to Triple A ball, but I guess they didn't have room for me. I told them to release me if they were not going to bring me up, and they did.

My career ended with a few games the next year with Kansas City. I went to spring training with them, began the season at Triple A, and was brought up in May. I threw in Yankee Stadium. I was having trouble with my arm. My shoulder was hurting. I got out of the inning, and the next day they released me. I had torn a bicep tendon, and that was it. I would have needed another surgery and, truth be told, mentally I had had enough. I thought it was time to find something else to do. I was 32.

In hindsight, I see that when the Phillies traded me, it just sucked all the desire out of me. I just had the best year of my career, and I was on a team that I loved with a great manager. We went to the World Series. We lost. Some might say, *I lost*. Either way, I couldn't wait to get back there next year.

I had the best year of my life and got traded for it. That's when the game became nothing but a business for me. Basically, I got traded for one pitch. After Ralph Terry gave up that homer to Bill Mazeroski in the 1960 World Series, he didn't get traded. Two years later, he was the ace of the staff and *won* the seventh game. I didn't get that chance.

The Phillies front office said it was because they thought my best years were behind me. I had one year left on my contract. I wished they had given me the chance to find out. They made the decision they thought they needed to make, and I can respect that. As soon as I was traded, that's when baseball became just a job. I just didn't have it in me to work as hard as you have to work to compete. I just wasn't into it anymore. Their opinion that my best years were behind me became a self-fulfilling prophecy. I don't know if that would have been true if I had stayed with the Phillies. No one will ever know.

I believe in my heart to this day that I got traded because the owners thought the fans would crucify me the next year. They underestimated the fans of Philadelphia. They underestimated me. They didn't understand that the fans appreciated that I didn't run and hide after the game or during the off-season. They miscalculated the relationship I had and still have with the fans.

When Houston came to Philadelphia in May, I walked out of the dugout and the fans gave me a standing ovation. They had figured it out. They knew that I was a guy who fit into their city. They knew that every day I walked out there I gave everything I had. They understood that a player can lose a game and wear the goat horns, but they got past it. The Phillies' fans are fanatics, but they aren't crazy. They know the game and understood. I wish the Phillies owners and front office had known their fans better and known me better.

The first thing I did after I retired was nothing. It was also the second. I did nothing for quite awhile, just stayed home and played with the kids. I remarried right after the World Series in 1993. I now have five children. Doing nothing to excess is not unusual for players when they first leave the game. It is not something I recommend. Once your career is over, it is better to find something pretty quick. Most of us don't.

There is nothing new about this. Talk to players from any era, and most of them will tell you the transition to normal life after being a big-league ballplayer is tough. John Blanchard, who passed away in 2009, didn't play all that long and was never a regular. But he played for the 1961 Yankees and hit two home runs in the World Series that year, so he had some major memories.

He had some major post-baseball adjustment problems, too, including developing a drinking problem. He just didn't know what to do with himself for a long time. He finally got it under control, found a new career, and enjoyed returning for Yankees Old Timers games, but he learned the hard way that you just can't keep doing what you did as a player in any way, shape, or form. Some guys today, just like Johnny, have their entire identities wrapped up in being a ballplayer. It's tough when you finally have to be something else.

Jackie Jensen was the American League Most Valuable Player in 1958, but he just didn't like the lifestyle: the traveling, the constant focus of the media, what it did to family life. After the next year, in which he hit 28 homers and drove in 112, he retired at age 32. As it turned out, he discovered he wanted back in the game. But after sitting out a year, he had lost his edge. He played one more year with mediocre results then retired for good. Years later, when he was a middle-aged high school baseball coach, he was most regretful for not appreciating his baseball career when he had it.

Think about it. A very high number of American boys grow up wishing they could be professional athletes. Some have to give up that dream the first time they step on the field or court. The game tells them early and often to find another dream.

For others it lasts longer, maybe through high school or college. But only a small number of guys who sign professional contracts make the major leagues. Those of us who have careers of any length are still dreaming in a way. The longer you live the dream, the harder it is to wake up.

Salaries today, and even when I played, allow a certain amount of time to adjust and figure things out. But no matter how much money you have, you are not going to be happy in your life if you are not engaged in something. Ballplayers have to be so focused and intense during the season that is it truly difficult for us to find anything later in life that comes close.

Mickey Mantle said that after he retired, he would dream he was outside Yankee Stadium. He would try every door but none would open. You don't have to be a shrink to figure that one out.

I never had a dream about baseball until I retired, either. Sure, I daydreamed about playing; every kid does. But a real dream while I was asleep, no. After I quit, I began to have dreams that I was still playing. I'm on the mound. I don't remember the situation, what team I'm on or who we are playing. It is just the fact that I *am* playing. Then I wake up, and I'm disappointed. I still have that dream a lot.

Maybe I have it because I feel that I could have played longer. Then again, it could just be the plain longing to do what was so much fun in my youth. I think most people have this sort of dream. Mine just happens to take place on a major-league pitching mound.

One thing I never did dream about was that pitch to Joe Carter. Not the next day, not the next week, and not to this day. I'm told that when a person deals with issues in real life, they don't get haunted by their dreams. So the pummeling I took in front of my locker that night may have saved me a few nightmares. Lord knows I see enough replays of it that I shouldn't have to dream about it, too.

I was never one to seek the spotlight, so I never missed that part of it. But you do get used to living a lifestyle that is almost impossible to maintain after you retire. Sure, we sat down with my agent for years before I quit, making a plan for retirement, but the reality is different. In order to make your money last, there must be major adjustments. They might not have seemed so drastic when they were five, 10 years in the future. But when the future is now, it can hit pretty hard. You can tell yourself you are going to cut down after you retire, but doing it is another matter. I'll be the first one to tell you I didn't do a very good job of it.

I enjoyed all my free time, sure. I had a couple of buddies back in Texas. When I wasn't at home, I was with them on the golf course. We had a 600-acre ranch down there. I fell in love with the slower pace of life down there when I was with the Rangers. It's quiet. Well, maybe not as quiet for me as for some others. As a hobby, I took up team roping.

When a man retires from a stressful career of opposing other men who hold large wooden clubs and desire only to damage your reputation; when a man earns his living in a way that elicits strong emotional reactions from tens of thousands of people, whose approval can turn instantly from adulation to revulsion based on whether a ball is caught in front of a fence or behind it, that man needs an active challenge even after retirement.

A steer flies out of a rodeo shute, two riders in hot pursuit. They try to rope and stop the steer as quickly as possible. The team that does it quickest wins. I found it severely addictive. I love golf, but that little ball just sitting there was not a sufficient outlet for my adrenaline, not after a decade or so of ninth innings.

My ranch was about 20 miles from Stephenville, Texas, the Cowboy Capital of the World, in case you didn't know. It is also home to the Eagles' No. 1 draft choice of 2007, former University of Houston quarterback Kevin Kolb. I gradually made friends with Ron Pack and Tuff Hedeman, who are bull riders and business associates. Tuff is a four-time World Champion Bull Rider, so yeah, he's like the Randy Johnson or Willie Mays of bull riders. I started out playing golf with them. They taught me to rope and got me started.

My best friend back in Oregon when I was growing up had horses, and I rode with him. Since I was a kid, all I really wanted was to have a big piece of property and have horses and other animals. When I bought the ranch, I started riding again, then started herding on some of the bigger ranches near mine, and that led to the roping and rodeos.

We roped at our ranches and went to competitions. We went to the U.S.A. finals in Oklahoma City every year to watch the best and compete. I won five or six belt buckles, a saddle, and some money.

Team roping is like baseball in that they don't care who you are or where you come from, you just have to be able to get the job done. There are different classifications. You get a number from one to five. A number one is a novice. The higher your number, the more skilled you are. You add your number to your teammate's, then enter competition against teams with the same total number.

Age is not much of a factor. You can do it for a long time. My usual teammate is nine years older than me. But it can get a little humbling. Down in Texas and Oklahoma, the kids grow up with ropes in their hands. That's all they do. It is very possible that you can get into a competition, feel all *macho* and capable, and get the crap kicked out of you by a seven-year-old.

It was fun, but it wasn't like I was going to be a star on the rodeo circuit. Whatever your nest egg, if you are not adding to it, it goes down pretty fast. I never got down to zero, but it got to the point where it was slapping me in the face. I wasn't socially isolated. I wasn't depressed. But I needed to know, "What's next?"

I eventually sold the ranch and moved back to the Philadelphia area. Texas just didn't have any kind of job or career possibilities for me. I reached out to develop the contacts I had made with the Phillies.

I sent out a resume to every big-league team. But when you have the nickname "Wild Thing," I found out there aren't too many teams in a hurry to have you work with their young pitchers.

I finally caught on as the pitching coach with a Class A independent league team in Atlantic City. After a year and a half, they fired the manager and I replaced him. I had a great time managing. I even started a few games. One day our starter couldn't go, so I went out and flipped a few sliders. I walked a lot fewer batters in the Atlantic League than I did in the National League, but I labored under no illusions.

When the team folded, I tried to get back into organized baseball. I got one interview, as a minor league pitching coach with the Phillies. They decided they wanted to go with someone with more experience, which I had a hard time understanding. I had 16 years as a player, three as a coach and manager. Somehow I didn't fit with what they were trying to do.

I had to let go of thinking that I might get back between the lines. My nickname was a barrier everywhere I went. I've had people tell me that organizations thought I was the type of wild guy who wouldn't show up on time, not follow the rules. Hey, the only wild thing about me was that I had trouble finding the strike zone on occasion. I never had trouble finding my way back to my room before curfew, or the way to the locker room. I've never been late for anything in my life. I take what I do for a living very seriously. I'm not going to steal anybody's money. If somebody is paying me to do a job, I'm going to do it the best I can. If teams had taken the time to get to know me, given me a real interview, they might have realized that I do understand the game.

Be careful of the nickname you might acquire. It can stay with you, and there might be a time you wish you didn't have it. I never minded being called Wild Thing when I played. I don't now. It's kind of how I've become known. But I think part of it now is that fans know I'm not wild in what I say about the game.

I worked for casinos in Atlantic City for a while. For a short time, John Kruk and I had a little local television show in Philadelphia, but it didn't go anywhere. Then Angelo Cataldi, who has owned Philadelphia radio sports talk for years, had me on his show. It went over pretty well I guess because I didn't die after we lost the World Series. They offered me a regular spot there. Then I went on the daily news show with Comcast and did a pregame and postgame show. I now do "The Wild Pitch" on WPHT-AM in Philadelphia, and this spring I started on MLB-TV. And of course, there is this book you are reading.

There is also Wild Thing Southpaw Salsa, our family blend that has become pretty popular. It started out as something my wife and daughter and I made up in our kitchen simply because we couldn't find any salsa to buy that we really liked. My favorite class in high school was cooking class, and I've always enjoyed messing in the kitchen. My years in Texas gave me a taste for what I consider real salsa. I talked about it some on the radio. A food broker called and said he wanted to represent us. It took off from there.

It's made down in San Antonio now according to the recipe we created in our kitchen. It comes in both wild and mild. The mild sells more, probably because most of our sales are in the northeast. When we get big in Texas, I suspect the wild will sell a little better.

You can't really retire at 32, no matter how much money you have. Once you wake up from the major-league dream, there is still a lot of life left to live.

It's fun doing the writing and broadcasting. If it isn't quite as much fun as striking out a guy to get a save, then at least it's never as awful as when that same guy puts your fastball into the upper deck.

Chapter Seven

Life with a Microphone

Being part of the media means that you become part of the public relations efforts of baseball, whether you like it or not. It is the same with the players. Everywhere you go, fans are going to relate their experience with you to their overall feelings about the game. I think players in general need to make themselves a little more accessible to the fans—come out and sign autographs before the game and all. Give back a little and spend more time with kids and the average fans. Teams ought to encourage this. I don't know how it is now, but no team ever asked me to go out a little early and sign. I just did it. It's up to the player.

For decades, kids could come down close to the field before the game for photographs and autographs. Now I hear that some teams won't let anybody down there unless they have a ticket for those seats. It also used to be that hardcore fans would come out for batting and fielding practice. They would have been at the ballpark for a couple of hours before the game even started. Now a lot of the teams don't even have the park open for practice. Security, I guess. Too bad, because seeing the players at practice, in that more relaxed environment, was another way for fans to relate more to the players as people.

I threw out the first pitch before Game 1 of the NLDS between the Phillies and the Brewers in 2008. (AP Images)

Otherwise, I think Major League Baseball is doing a pretty good job of marketing itself these days, which hasn't always been true. For years, the sole idea of marketing for many teams was to open the gates and sell tickets. I do think there are some cities that are struggling to maintain their fan base. The best marketing is winning. There isn't a team in baseball that can't improve its bottom line with a few more wins.

Baseball has done a better job than other major-league sports at keeping its games available to the average family. There was a big furor over the $2,000 tickets at the new Yankee Stadium when it opened in 2009. After the seats didn't sell, the price was cut in half. It didn't seem like much of a bargain at $1,000. I wonder what laws of supply and demand they were following?

Still, the price of anything is only expensive if you can't afford it or don't want to. There are seats in every ballpark that most people can afford, and baseball needs to keep it that way. Every player knows that some of the greatest fans are in the bleachers.

That's why I'll never support any plan to move the playoffs or World Series games to a warm-weather site. I think the fans that spend all year (or their whole lives!) rooting for their team deserve to be the host when their team gets to the postseason. Even for fans who don't attend the games, there is a whole experience of having those games in your city that should not be taken away.

Yes, the weather can be terrible in an East Coast or Midwest city at the end of October. But I think that is an acceptable price to pay to reward the fans in those cities. There is a home-field advantage that is important to postseason teams, too, and it is not just the chance to bat last. Teams are created with certain home parks in mind, and warm-weather sites would take away an advantage earned over a very long season.

The extra layer of playoffs created by the wild card contributes to pushing the World Series a little more toward winter, but again,

I think the price is worth the reward. The wild card keeps the season more interesting longer for more teams.

Baseball is different from other sports in that a lesser team will beat the better one far more often that in any other sport. That's one of the things that makes baseball great. You are only as good as your starting pitcher. So yes, a wild-card team that won 85 games has a good chance of beating a team that won 105 in a short series. But that was always true. The best team didn't always win the World Series, even before the playoffs. When the Pirates beat the Yankees in 1960, few thought the Pirates were better.

Nobody *anywhere* thought the 1969 Mets were better than the Orioles. These upsets are some of the most famous stories in baseball. The wild card just gives opportunities for more great stories. The team with the hot pitchers will win. Always have. Always will.

Baseball has usually been very slow to change. Baseball will discuss something for years, as though any little change will completely distort everything in the future and destroy everything in the past. Then, once the change happens, it's like the game had never been any different.

Take instant replays, for example. Baseball was years and years behind other sports in this area. Then they approved using it for home-run calls, and nobody even thinks about it any more. It's just a good idea whose time came about 20 years ago. Twenty years late is about par for changes in baseball. The whole idea is just to get it right. Humans are fallible, and yes, umpires are human. If you can plainly see it on the tape, call it right.

It's like the home-plate umpire using the first-base umpire for advice on checked swings. For years, umpires agreed that this was the hardest call they had to make. So why make it alone? If you watch taped games from years past, you never see umps ask for advice. Now they confer frequently. It makes for a better game for everybody.

I would not expand the use of instant replay, however. Plays at the plate, tags on the bases, and bang-bang plays at first are just not that obvious. They depend a lot on the perspective. A lot of times I see a replay on television and from one camera he looks safe, and from another he looks out. On those, I think you have to go with the umpire. That's why when you see a manager arguing with umpires, he is likely complaining that the ump was out of position, pleading that from the *correct* position a different conclusion would surely be drawn.

Among the other recent changes in the game, using the All-Star Game to determine the home-field advantage in the World Series is a little flawed in my opinion. Yes, it increases interest for fans and players alike. But it is so obvious to me—if the game is going to mean something, you can't play it like an exhibition game.

I made the All-Star Team once, in 1989. The first guy I faced was Ruben Sierra. I had left Texas that year and joined the Cubs. Ruben and I had been teammates for four years, going back to Double A and moving right up to the bigs. He was the fastest guy I ever saw going from first to third. If you threw him strikes, you could get him out. If you threw him bad pitches, he would kill 'em. What a great bad-ball hitter! You could not throw a ball low enough to him when he hit righty. He'd pick it off his shoe tops and line it off the wall.

I walked him. Then I picked him off. He'd only seen my pickoff move for four years. I can understand why he hadn't quite solved it yet. It was a thrill being picked for the team, and I am glad that you see guys happy to play in it now rather than complaining about not getting three days off, as it seemed some guys used to do every year.

You could still have the fans vote for the players, but the managers ought to be able to decide who is starting and at what position, and for how long. And you probably don't want to pinch-hit for Albert Pujols in the seventh inning of a one-run game, or whatever.

The greater problem you have is with the pitching. Now a pitcher goes at most two innings and most of them just one. Nobody has to miss a turn because of their All-Star Game efforts. If you are really playing to win, some manager might want to pitch a guy three innings. If he struggles a little, throws a lot of pitches, he might miss a start. That is not going to go down so well with that pitcher's team.

Suppose the game is tight and somebody decides a closer should go two innings, somebody like Mariano Rivera. When he goes for more than one now, New York fans reacts as they do on a 300-point dip of the Dow Jones—like a potential disaster lies ahead. There seems to be a gentlemen's agreement on these things now, but it is an agreement that is based on a contradiction, an exhibition game where it matters who wins.

Of course, All-Star Games have been perilous even decades before they determined anything about the World Series. Dizzy Dean had his toe broken by a line drive off the bat of Indians slugger Earl Averill in 1937. Pete Rose's home-plate crash at the plate broke Ray Fosse's collarbone in 1970. Both Dean and Fosse were never the same. In fact, you risk injury *more* if you try to let up.

The same problem, in a way, comes up with the World Baseball Classic. I'm a big fan of it. I think it's great for baseball. I know, as a player, if they had asked me to represent my country, I would have been honored. I understand why guys want to play.

But it does put people into compromising positions. I believe that a player has a commitment to the team that has his name on a contract. What if I get hurt? I'm surprised it hasn't already come up more than it has. I know that the Mets seemed to think that

Oliver Perez played for Mexico in the 2009 World Baseball Classic. Did his participation make him less prepared for his duties with the Mets? (AP Images)

Oliver Perez started the 2009 season less prepared that he should have due to playing for Mexico. He only pitched twice in 19 days, so he wasn't really in shape when he reported to the team that had just signed him to a three-year contract for $36 million.

Even worse, he threw 85 pitches in his second and last WBC start, which isn't much for June but is way more than he would have thrown in a comparable spring-training game. You can't say for sure that the WBC washed out Perez's season, but you can't ignore what happened, either.

Likewise, Dice-K helped Japan's WBC team a lot more than he helped the Red Sox in 2009. The guy with the self-proclaimed indestructible arm found out differently. This stuff is only going to get worse if something isn't done.

The timing now just isn't right. They don't want it right after the season because everybody is tired. They don't want it in the middle of winter, because nobody is game-ready. So it's held during spring training, but it's not a substitute for spring training. A player is not going to work on his delivery or practice pulling more or hitting the other way when he is trying to win a championship for his country. He's not going to say, "No more than 50 pitches for me today." He's not going to work on playing a new position.

I'd like to see them play the WBC with amateurs. Personally, I'd like it more that way. College players and other amateurs would have time to prepare for it. While it would generate less interest because of the lack of major leaguers, it would also create interest in those players who excelled.

*　*　*

I didn't set out to have a career in media. Once I got the microphone in front of me, I just talked about what I saw on the field, and the career developed from there. I try to treat players the way I wanted to be treated when I played. I don't do a lot of interviews, and when I do, I want it to be quick: get to the point, get the answer, and get out. I don't ask anything personal because I don't care about a player's personal life. The key is to never forget that I played the game. I try not to make too much of things. I just want to watch a baseball game and say the same things I would have said if I were watching from the bullpen.

Everybody who has played knows how the game is supposed to be played. Any player who is honest with himself is not going to question what I've said. You can't attack a guy if he makes a mistake or question his desire or his makeup. You can say, "That's the way the play should have been made," because the player knows that, and nobody can do it right every time. But don't make it personal.

Fans and reporters who didn't play major-league ball often don't realize just how difficult the game is. If it were easy, a lot more people would be playing. A fan might love baseball because he played Little League or high school or college ball. The big leagues might look like the same game, and in a way it is, of course. But in some very important ways, it is an entirely different game, too. For one, it is now the player's profession, and also, the guys you are playing with and against are the best in the world. Unless you've been in the dugout, it is hard to comprehend the amount of focus, skill, and consistent performance required.

I have not had players take offense with me. Nope. I will never say, "He looked lazy," or question a player's integrity or commitment. I don't believe in that. I take it as a given that every player is trying to do his job.

You can say that a player doesn't have enough range, but you can't say a guy is dogging it on the field because you can't get into another man's head. That's the problem the umpires have now with giving warnings on inside pitches. They are supposed to judge intent. That's impossible. At best it's a guess, and you should not be guessing another man's intention. You end up with warnings being given when batters get hit with breaking balls. That's just stupid.

You can say, "It didn't look like he busted on that play," if that's what you saw when a guy gets thrown out trying to stretch a single and you saw him loping out of the box. But you cannot say, "He should have run faster," because you do not know for sure if he was truly capable of running faster, given all the variables on every play. That's how commentators get into trouble with players.

I'm not going to sugarcoat things, but the one thing I will never do is attack a player personally. That's not my job. My job is to say what I see on the field. Fans might not know it, but I'm a reporter.

One thing I have discovered going from working every Phillies game to working on MLB-TV, where I might be asked to comment on any team at any time, is that you can't possibly know what is going on with every team. So it becomes even more important to just say what you see. You don't know the background of every player. Even if you read the press release from a team's media office and it says, "Joe Shortstop was hit on the hand last night and is day to day," what do you really know? Or you might know that a player is recently off the disabled list, recovering from this or that, but you still don't know anything because one player might need to be 100 percent before he comes back and another may be too eager and come back too soon. Just say what you see.

I'm thinking of the fan sitting at home who might not know all of the finer points of how every play ought to be made. I'm going to tell him what should have happened on that play, whether it did or not. Whether or not the guy was hustling is not my call. I can only say that this is where the throw should have gone, or this is where the guy should have been. He was either there or he wasn't. He either made the tag, or he missed it.

I can go down on the field and talk to the players, managers, and coaches, but the bottom line of my job is to report. Period. Most of the guys in uniform are pretty slick about saying as little as possible, anyway. With so many different kinds of media today, and really, not everybody covering baseball knowing all that much about the game, I don't blame the players for sticking to clichés.

The broadcasters I can't stand are the former players who have forgotten that they played and made every mistake that they now knock the current players for making. You have to temper your criticism with a little humility. That's true in every profession.

It's been easy for me because I'll never forget I was a player. There was never going to be a writer or broadcaster who was going to be harder on me than I was on myself. I threw balls that got hit into the cheap seats—or at least they used to be cheap seats. I knew why it happened. I never made excuses. The Phillies pitching staff started out 2009 by giving up an amazing number of home runs—40 in their first 20 games. Point blank you can say why: location. You throw it down the middle to big-league hitters, and they are going to drive it a long way. Period. I know it. The Phillies know it. They aren't going to get hacked at me because they know I am just reporting what is going on. It helps that they know I made every mistake that they are making. And several they haven't gotten around to yet.

Acknowledgments

I'd like to acknowledge Charlie Hough, Dickie Noles, and Larry Parrish for taking time to talk to a hyperactive 21-year-old rookie and teach me the right way to play this game!

—Mitch Williams

Thanks to John Monteleone for guiding me through the co-creation of this book from beginning to end, and to the Larry Ritter Memorial Lunch Bunch for providing friendship, support, and baseball wit and wisdom since 1991.

—Darrell Berger